WALKING IN
YOUR POWER

With LOVE
Barbara Derrick
2017

WALKING IN YOUR POWER

Lessons From the Grandmothers

Barbara M. Derrick

Walking in Your Power

Copyright © 2017 by Barbara M. Derrick

Published by
Native Studio Art
www.nativestudioart.net

Publishing consultant
Professional Woman Publishing, LLC
www.pwnbooks.com

ISBN: 978-0-9958642-1-4

Dedicated to You
May the stories from Walking in Your Own Power
Bring joy, laughter and healing
Creativity Never Sleeps
Creator continues to breathe color into your life's canvas

CONTENTS

INTRODUCTION

I've put together this book to use as a workbook. There are 13 chapters (representing 13 large segments on the back of every turtle.) The turtle's attributes are in dedication and honor of an elder who mentored me over the course of ten years of my life. Rather than taking each segment and talking about the moon teachings and its original lessons, I've embodied seven teaching subtitles of the "Women's Round" within 7 different chapters: Mother, Dawn Star, Morning Star, Grandmother Within, Mother Earth, Child Within and the Moon. You will find its subtitle in all chapters under the chapter title in brackets, e.g. (Mother). Four chapters highlight the four directions: Spiritual-East, Emotional-South, Physical-West and Mental-North. The last two chapters: – Woman-Muskwa and Man-Father for a total of 13. *See Appendix A for diagram.*

Reading each chapter, you will experience life through the eyes of a young elder named "Muskwa" (Cree for Bear). She came to me from a dream and she carries the messages contained within this book. I honor the spirit of Muskwa, she is the spirit of my clan. When she arrived in my dream it was at a time in my life when great change was occurring—I was breaking many different cycles of abuse.

During the writing of my coauthored chapter titled "Muskwa Walks" in First Lady Nation, Vol IV and the writing of this book "Walking in Power", my mother passed away quite suddenly in January 24th, 2016. I dedicate the grizzly bear to her, as I see my late mother smiling back at me from the heavens. There is an old photo of her when she was 16 years old, fresh out of Residential School with that sly look about her, quietly sitting on horse tack and rope. She was a woman who was not only physically strong but who inwardly "forged steel." In this book, Muskwa shares her tears, fears, anger and tribulation in various chapters and not to be thought of as her continued "resentment." Instead, the character steps forward to share from a place that will help readers begin to look at their own stories as a pathway to their own healing and inner wisdom to "let go, let God."

Bear spirit or Muskwa introduced me to my family's Tshilqot'in traditional practices, belief and customs. In my language we say "bear" as "Ses." From the mountains I was drawn to the prairies to seek out the answers in healing myself. Through these teachings I was connected to the ancestors or "eswydan" (e-swi-dan) and some of the clues they left along the historical trails. Signs etched in rock, and stone formations contained ancestral family lineage that helped put the pieces of the puzzle together. Once, we as a people consisted of family groups who were recognized for certain functions in the community. The arrangement of the clans created harmony in political, social, pharmaceutical and judicial aspects of the people. There were a number of clans, each with a special role in protocols, decision-making processes, and the management of all matters. This list is but a small fragment of the clans, but it will give you an idea of the structure that was in place long before the Europeans arrived.

Bear: healers, peacemakers, justice and policing
Bird: visionaries, gave direction and provided the big picture to the people
Small four legged: (i.e. wolf) protectors of the women and children
Larger four legged: (buffalo, horse) were warriors
Water species: Turtle – spiritual leader and mediator. When consulted upon concerns, all was carefully weighed and then a final decision was made. The Turtle got the "last say" during discussions

that had no direction. I've heard other tribes have given the sturgeon or the salmon this seat within the western part of Canada. I think the most important part of our heritage is getting past disagreements about who is right or who is wrong, and release the need to control information among one another in reclamation of our ancestral practices.

In the past we had family groupings referred to as "Clans," but there was also a name giving process intact. Unlike its Christian counterpart, a name held the energy of the person's alignment with a particular spirit. A child would receive a name at birth; if the mother had a son, the father would name him according to the first thing that he saw; if she had a daughter, she would pick a name in much the same way. Looking out into the natural environment that surrounded them, the parents found names to guide their children. In the early 1800s a baby girl who was born into our family, was given the name Tlo'isdan (Tlo-eee-sdan) meaning "Mountain Sweetgrass." She would later become known to us as one of my grandmother's sisters. It is important to note that at the time there were very few recordings in the Catholic tomes of any of our relatives with their traditional names intact, as it was the practice to obliterate the "Indian in the child." As a reader, you will become familiar with the given names through the characters: Red Tree, Big Rock etc., contained within the pages of this book.

Muskwa's stories not only touch upon wisdom and insight, but also provide transformational energy for you as the reader to create empowerment within your life. She will lend you courage in locating your own answers on this spiritual journey. Completing the activities at the end of each chapter will help get you started in the healing of your paradigms or learning models blocking your personal expression so that you can "Walk in Your Own Power."

In order for you to get the most out of the exercises, I suggest doing each exercise according to the 21-day habit forming theory practice described in "Psycho Cybernetics." In doing so, you will create or break a habit within 21 days. Perhaps you do better with a partner? Team up with one or more people who you know, and meet once a week to share with each other.

I believe this book is for you. You are a person who's seeking empowerment and I'm grateful to Creator for guiding you in reading my book.

ONE

FULL CIRCLE

Respirator & Silver Swans (Mother)

It was Friday, the day unfolded much like any other day. A young elder named Muskwa moved about her day following her business schedule. Most people Muskwa's age were focused on retirement, dreaming of their last day of work and its transportation into a sedentary way of living. She noted people believed in the land of milk and honey; a place where there would be no more work, no more money worries, a pension to support their travels, and future luxuries. The meaning of retirement meant something different to her; she had simply "withdrawn from her professional career" to follow her dream, on her own terms. Since her departure from employment she had discovered a renewed joy in her own creativity. Each day she looked forward to her office where her memoirs developed into pages, which began to show promise. When she was in her art studio she felt shrouded by creativity, it called to her soul, she acknowledged it as the "spirit spark," a universal ingredient to help motivate herself and others to become the best version of themselves.

On this particular day, Muskwa's writing took her into her residential school experience and the memory had slowed her down. She struggled emotionally to continue writing. She acknowledged how vulnerable she was at nine years old, and the feelings of abandonment that came from an experience so long ago. While she was deeply immersed in translation of the feelings into words on paper, anger surfaced. Muskwa was appalled at the magnitude of genocidal destruction on her people. First, the religious indoctrination to 'kill the Indian in the child', through a series of spiritual, mental, emotional, physical and sexual abuses in a school setting. She imagined her mother leaving the residential school at sixteen years old with bottled up untold truths. Muskwa was told her mother entered residential school at the age of nine years old, until she became sixteen years old. A lot of years went by, and the three monkeys, 'see no evil, hear no evil, and feel no evil' seemed a fitting analogy of her mother's survival of the residential school system.

At sixteen years old, her mother was free to leave the school and to go back home into her own community. She arrived home with three monkeys of silence on her shoulders that would eventually begin to rob her mother's mental, emotional, physical, spiritual and psychological forces. Holding secrets meant finding a way to forget. Eventually her mother's active role in life would be whittled down to the alcohol. There were warning signs along the way as Muskwa was growing up, but nothing could prepare her for her mother's loss of her father who passed away one morning in early June from stomach cancer. What followed was her mother's increased desire to drink, and many days Muskwa remembered the empty house, watching her own dad Stone Man pace the floor with worry in his heart.

The year Red Tree's father passed away would be the same year her parents separated and her mother obtained custody. Muskwa and her late brother were placed into residential schooling that fall. Muskwa remembered the day clearly. It was Halloween when her father found out where they had been placed.

Muskwa straightened her dress, and repositioned herself on her chair. She acknowledged "forgiveness," she would change the "bitterness," mix it with the sweet love of spirit, and allow old wounds like this one to flow into the ocean of love and mercy. She took a deep breath, filled her mind with love. Then she enveloped all her resentful thoughts in white light. Closing her eyes, she brought the light into her being; it felt so right.

She was in deep in the space when the phone rang. Muskwa jumped up and then answered her phone in an awkward manner. "Hello," she said with a gruff voice. The voice on the other end said, "Please sit down." Muskwa's heart skipped a beat, and her adrenaline went up a notch. "What? What is it? What's wrong?" This would be the phone call that would change her life, and tilt the axis of her world. "It's your mother, she's in ICU. You need to come home." It was an all too familiar phone call, one that resonated with the loss of her brother a few years back. Muskwa fought through her tears, she was in shock! Her head felt numb, her motions robotic as she fought disbelief. It was late, a fresh snow and high wind warnings for the highway had been petitioned by the road service application, and she decided to wait and leave in the morning.

The morning saw Muskwa as she sped down the highway, and a recent phone call confirmed Red Tree's prognosis went from stable to acute. With mounting grief, she stepped on the gas. Flying down January roads that were covered in thawing fresh snow was crazy and the black on the road's shoulders became an obvious threat when her rear wheels slightly swerved and grabbed her attention.

All of a sudden she psychically heard, "let go, let God!" As the tears cascaded down her cheeks she saw something large move on a fence post to her right. She quickly looked, and a bald eagle lifted itself from the post into the air. The eagle swooped above the car so close that Muskwa swore she could almost touch the feathers. She acknowledged it was her mother sending a message, and then she slowed the car down. "What a profound message; bald eagles don't hang out during winter do they?" she thought to herself.

Peacefulness embraced her as she arrived and parked the car in hospital parkade. She found her way to the 'Intensive Care Unit' to find her mother Red Tree still holding on. The next twelve hours crawled by in a blur; nurses and doctors became a source of information, comfort and support for Muskwa. Her mother's prognosis was dim; at first a pancreatic infection had been diagnosed. Her symptoms had started out with high blood pressure, which now skyrocketed. In an attempt to help her breathe, she was hooked up to a breathing machine. In the corner just behind the bed, Muskwa counted as many as ten bags of fluid, all hooked individually to the IV rack. Such a large number of medications administered to her mother was proof of a medical team's effort to help her mother's body heal. Time slowly passed as Muskwa sat beside her mother's bed, numb and almost paralyzed with disbelief, seeing her mother here at this moment in time. Was it a nightmare? She queried herself. That evening the doctor told Muskwa a decision needed to be made by her and the family. According to new medical information, a piece of Red Tree's bowel had broken off into her bloodstream, and there was nothing more the medical team could do for her. It would be time to call family and prepare for Red Tree's life to end.

Muskwa felt empty and devoid of feelings. She didn't know what to think, and the feeling of freaking out overwhelmed her. She resisted the urge to scream out her grief and pain. The feeling of hopelessness cascaded over her as she prepared for her mother's translation into the afterlife. She sat holding her mother's right hand, watching her mother's chest rise and fall. Tracing the veins on her mother's hand, Muskwa was taken to a past memory of her childhood when she was four years old. She was busy running her small fingers over her mother's hands, tracing the veins. Oh, how deeply she loved her mom! From her memory she heard Red Tree say, *"Stop that! You're going to shorten my life!"* Muskwa understood her mother's reaction later on in her adulthood as some superstitious cultural belief. In reaction to the memory she said aloud, *"pffffffffff."*

A noise sounded, "beep!" A nurse entered the ICU to recalibrate the machine where the medicines were being dispensed into her mother. No movement, just the sound of the breathing machine which was doing the breathing for her mother. Muskwa's eyes filled with tears as she looked at the screen that monitored her mother's blood pressure, heart beat and vital organs. Her eyes became fixed on the wavy green line, the yellow and red alternation of wave signals.

Muskwa shifted in her chair breathing deeply, wiping the tears from her face. She relaxed for a moment and more memories flooded into her consciousness. She saw herself and her mother in a Social Worker's office. They were signing adoption forms to give away Muskwa's newly born daughter to a good family. Arriving at the final decision had been heart breaking for both women and here they were sitting at the desk staring at the documents in front of them.

Internally Muskwa sobbed, her body was numb as feelings resonated with the loss she felt holding her mother's hand. From the past, she recalled summoning the courage to get through the emotional turmoil. In the lifetime of her past story, she recalled the tears and how they pooled behind her eyelids threatening to release down her cheeks. How she held her breath to block the emotional breakdown without passing out was a mystery. All she wanted was to be strong for God because at that moment there was nothing else. Muskwa didn't know where she learned to do this, but she shifted her attention onto an object to ground herself and then shut down the cascade of emotions. Above their heads was a sterling silver flying bird mobile, it was moving ever so slightly. The light hitting the chrome, the smoothness of the metal held her attention, and a feeling of peace swept over her.

Gratitude filled Muskwa's heart for a brief moment as she reflected on the "dragonfly child" coming home. Ten years ago she remembered reading a Sioux excerpt somewhere about adopted children looking for their parents. Was it a coincidence more drag-onflies hovered near her each summer she became closer to finding her daughter? They so reminded her of giggly little children! So colorful, they would dance and flit about her! Then that one day, that beautiful day Muskwa and Rainbow Woman were reunited on the telephone. Muskwa remembers sharing the experience with her mother, it brought a faint smile to her own face.

The thought brought her back to the last discussion she had with Red Tree just before Christmas. "How were the kids? What were the boys doing? How about the girls? And how is Rainbow Woman?" The tempo of the discussion went deeper during their visit as Red Tree said, *"I wish things could have been different. It was his fault! (Referring to an ex-husband) If I could turn back time. We should have just taken her and made a life!"* Quiet had filled her mother's small apartment, and Muskwa remembered her response. "Mom, it's ok. It was meant to be this way. It wasn't your fault. It wasn't anyone else's fault. She was raised by really good people and she's in our life now." An awareness of "forgiveness" in the conversation brought the feeling of peace between both of them.

"Beep!" The sound of the breathing machine jarred Muskwa back to the present! Through her tears she saw her mother Red Tree laying there peacefully. Was there a glow to her mother's face? Or was that a trickery of her own vision? Muskwa then felt her mother's presence but it didn't come from the alcohol ravaged body that laid on the hospital bed. Red Tree was in the room. Muskwa felt her mother's energy fill the room; it was comforting, and nurtured her senses spiritually. A strong feeling of coming full-circle permeated Muskwa's senses like the changing of seasons when birth and death connect.

Breathing in the love and an ambient presence of her mother, she heard her say, "I'll always be here for you now." Muskwa realized her fear of death was really about all the losses she that had in her life compounded over a series of time. It seemed like all her people could do after the travesty of European contact and residential schools, was to quickly forget and move on. During the times of assimilation, there was no time to take stock of life. Yet, here she was taking stock of her life and her mother's. Harvesting the good, the strength and wisdom of the women in her culture in her lifetime.

Muskwa grew tired and weary, and crawled onto a cot made by the nurses to rest for a few minutes. As she rested she drifted off, and reflected on her second oldest son. His arrival helped her mother forget the loss of the first child. Her memories shifted back and forth from the time of the adoption, to how uncanny it was to find herself making an almost similar decision about another's life—her mother's.

Red Tree was closer to leaving when the nurses awakened Muskwa from the slumber of the spirit walk with her mother. Watching her mother's gradual entry into the spirit world triggered feelings and remembrances of the days when she gave birth to her children. During the time before the births, here was an intangible anticipation, and subtle excitement that entered the room. She felt this now. Through the windows in her mother's hospital room the sun began to crest the horizon, and the color grey embodied the landscape. Muskwa's grandmothers taught her that when the eagle swoops down to gather prayers it would be during this time of the day. The nurse said, "It'll be anytime now. If you wish to be with her, I'll pull up the chair for you."

Muskwa moved to her mother's bedside, and sat closely to her. Holding her hand, watching the lines slowly disappearing she said to Red Tree, "I love you mom. Thank you for being my mother." Tears poured down her face. She saw a small movement of her mother's eyebrow. The lines on the breathing machine became smaller. A baby cried in ICU. Muskwa noticed the lines spike up on the breathing machine, then slowly disappear. Each time the baby cried, the lines spiked up weakly, then began to fade. As her mother walked away from the equipment that held her life, the lines spiked up illustrative of her looking back, and the gradual fading of them as she joined those on the other side.

The room was unimaginably quiet. There was no drama like the movies, no crash carts, no screaming nurses or running doctors. Just Muskwa and the morning sun as her mother left into light. It was 5:58 a.m.

Muskwa realized she had become a young elder within the very few minutes of her mother's death. She felt alone, with exceptions to her father Big Rock who was now a resident in a senior's home. As she drove away from the hospital it became more important than ever to share her experience and stories with the world. She refused to be oppressed! It was obvious to her now; she was successful in breaking the cycles of violence within her. There was no such thing as getting life perfect, only choices and the realization we are all here to fulfill our journey through our experiences in the Earth Walk.

Chapter Summary

Awareness and a lifetime of lessons became two-fold to Muskwa that morning. She imparts with you that healing is possible; it's in each and every one of us. We can create a legacy to be proud of. We can leave an inheritance for others to desire change, to break cycles of violence within their lives. Muskwa wanted to leave a legacy, not to simply accept her life! Part of her mother's life chapter had been written by the residential school system, and she wanted you, the reader to feel the authenticity of your own life because it hasn't been published yet.

When Muskwa arrived at her hotel, she rearranged the bed and lay down. Sleep did not come, only a strange silence. A profound message filtered into her mind just before she closed her eyes, "What did she want people to say about her mother's legacy? What about her own legacy?" The eulogy of our lives should be written, by none other than our selves. Don't let someone write it for you! You do have a legacy, you matter. John Maxwell said, *"When I picked up my pen I knew this, God is writing through me to you."*

Exercise

The focus of this exercise is being "heard." Too often we become so busy in our day-to-day activities that when we go to express ourselves no one is receiving the messages. With increased development in technologies, long schedules and other distractions, it's easy to say "I'm too busy! I don't have time!" Communication breakdown and misunderstandings go with the territory of being busy, but it's become our excuse. It's a must in generating healing and a clear channel to function adequately in our work, and within our families. Busy means amassing "unresolved" conflicts, Paul Martinelli. 2016 Turning Point said, *"How we do anything, is how we do everything."*

Thinking about the legacy you would like to leave for your family, friends or children. What do you want them to know? How has loss affected your life, and what lessons did you learn? How will you make a difference? You can achieve this through writing and "listening." John Maxwell says, *"If you desire to create a legacy, then you need to leave something in others."*

Step 1: Find yourself a journal, and for each week complete the following:

1   Accomplishments: What went well for you this week? What are you proud of?

2   Disappointments: What didn't go so well for you this week?

3   Solution: What will you do differently to change the outcome? Solutions? Then how will you celebrate your awareness around the resolution you've discovered?

Step 2: Find someone you can phone, or have a "coffee date" with each week. Better yet, partner up with a group. While doing this exercise ensure your phone is turned off and you are genuinely listening! This exercise works better when you can look the other person in the eyes while they are sharing with you.

TWO

RUNNING DOWN THE CORRIDOR

East Direction – Spiritual

A s the sun poured through the blinds in the living room, Muskwa busied herself about the house. For the month of April, Mother Earth and Father Sky poured mutual blessings upon all the people of the earth. The weatherman predicted temperatures would rise to thirty-three Celsius this day. Before sitting down, Muskwa opened the curtains with a wide grin. Such a beautiful day! Another day of gratitude on this earth walk she thought. With her cup of coffee in hand, she sat down in front of her computer to visit her friend's posts on social media. Quietly, she sipped her coffee and read through the various posts about new babies, an upcoming funeral, another about a relative heading for surgery. She noticed the frequency of adoptees posting their requests to find their mothers over the last week. "What a generational time change!" she thought to herself. Not more than three and a half decades ago most people had land line telephones, and from a post office mailed their letters out. It was a time when people went to the library to do their research. Looking for a phone number meant a painstaking search, flipping page after page of a three-inch telephone directory book for a phone number. It was a time when people prided themselves in memorizing and recalling numbers with ease, and for other's like Muskwa not the case. She found it easier to call the operator when she needed a phone number.

Then there was the radio, not everyone owned a phone. She recalled how her mother rushed to turn on the radio at certain times of the day to listen to the community bulletins! "To Mrs. Krimshaw, Mrs Krimshaw of Anaham Lake. Your son is in hospital, please call this phone number for more information…" Today, high speed internet and or Wi-Fi access has replaced the older do-it-yourself technologies.

All of a sudden in her mind's eye she saw a set of "rabbit ears" wrapped in tin foil. To get better reception on the television, the antenna was wrapped in tin foil. When the channel was hazy or not coming in, someone had to readjust the antenna. On most occasions, because she was the oldest child, her dad asked her to be the rabbit twin. "Move a little more that way, and stop! Now stay right there don't move," her dad would say.

The memories faded as her attention went back to the face of the young adoptee in the photo from the social media site. The adoptee's face triggered an age old memory of her own first pregnancy; she was five months along with her first born. She saw herself wearing a light sky blue ruffled baby doll nightie. How many years did that one January event traumatize her?

Muskwa couldn't believe it took twenty-one years to resolve it! Until that time each moment the memory floated to the surface, she busied herself to push it back into her psyche. For the first ten years she was able to shove it back further with the help of drugs and alcohol, then came a day when she made the decision to quit both.

For the next eleven years she kept herself busy so she wouldn't have to think about the "legs", a demon in disguise. Where it came from she didn't know. Perhaps from emotional trauma coming from her childhood? It was definitely something she couldn't share with just anyone! Now with the growth and healing of many years within her, she recognized the majority of her emotional trauma was passed down historically. Pieces of information didn't make sense until she was ready to look into it deeper. Muskwa recalled how a teacher said to her, *"After a healing transition, an awareness or understanding of the issue will make it clearer."* She remembers the time clearly when she reached an epiphany of the "running legs" and the fear of the dark disappeared.

Muskwa reverted back to the memory of the experience on that particular day in the past. In the unwed mothers' home, there were six one–person rooms, as well as two rooms big enough for two women. Fortunate to be assigned her own small room, it still reminded her of a modern day residential school dorm. The unwed mother's home was managed by a "house mother' who supervised chores and activities. Everyone was assigned a task each week: cooking for a week, dusting, vacuuming and/or cleaning of the bathrooms.

The unwed mother's home provided arrangements ideal and con-ducive to fostering healthy babies upon their arrival day. Although the atmosphere held little in terms of stress, the emotional roller coaster could be triggered by someone going into labour.

A baby's arrival meant a chain reaction of feelings as decisions to keep the child, or to adopt it out. Muskwa remembered as expectant dates drew closer so did the first time mother's stress, confusion, depression, and anger.

The arrival of the first baby was in October. Muskwa had only been at the unwed mother's home for a month. A thirty-five-year-old woman had her baby, was going to give it up for adoption, then decided against the decision. Muskwa recollected how the woman brought her baby boy to the house to say good-bye to everyone. Oh, how it triggered a month of angered reaction amidst the nine remaining young women, including herself!

Living in the same house with nine other pregnant women created its challenges. In the morning a line up started in the bathroom. With nine women in a rush to use the bathroom, laundry room or kitchen, it was going to create a certain amount of stress. Before she knew it nine o'clock would arrive, and a curfew followed with lights off!

There Muskwa would sit with a small desk lamp on, studying. It was her goal to catch up on two months of backed up homework. Prior to arriving she had dropped out of most of her classes in school. Working through the long distance learning modules she was determined to complete her grade ten before her baby was born.

Through study, she escaped her physical dilemma, emotional abandonment, mental judgement of herself, and the rejection she felt from her family. When she opened her module, a new world unfolded before her, new possibilities, and new insights. Once her pen hit paper and her eyes affixed on the words, she became completely immersed. The level of focus was equivalent to the amount of emotional/mental pain she experienced during the day. Focus became more acute when there was negativity from the young women in the house, or a call from an unsupportive family member that she wanted to forget. She downloaded all of it into her study.

That one evening Muskwa recanted from her memory, while sitting at the desk she was very focused. Laughter echoed from the hallway, then silence. All of a sudden the tranquility was broken by running and squealing followed by muffled laughter.

The noise pulled Muskwa from the rhythm of her concentration. "EEEEEEEKKKKK!" The shrieks filled the corridor and then more laughter from the bathroom. Muskwa was really irritated. "Stop it! ha ha ha ha," came the voice of one woman. To Muskwa it sounded like two women were splashing water at one another. "How immature!" she thought to herself. Despite the noise, she tried to go back to her module. She summoned how difficult it was for her to find the zone, and overriding the irritation took a minute. Then she found herself drifting into place, and as she arrived in her focused space she clearly recalled thinking to herself, "If a ghost snuck up behind you, I would love to see you both run!" The satisfaction was plastered all over her face in a weak smile. The shift back to her focus was ever so subtle and then screams filled the corridor!

Muskwa was bolted back to reality, "What?" She heard running feet, and then crying. "What a bunch of spoiled brats! Why did you have an argument?" she thought. She recollected turning the desk lamp off to remain undiscovered by the house mother. There was a din of silence for a few minutes. Her memory shifted to the voices on the other side of her door in the hallway. "Who was in the hallway?" She thought to herself. She saw herself inching closely to the door as she listened. Familiar voices from the young women filtered through the unopened door. Muskwa opened the bedroom door, and there stood four women. Two were hysterical and the other two were listening to the story. As she inched herself into the circle, it wasn't long before all eight other women and the house mother were together in the same spot. The house mother quickly calmed the hysteria building within the circle of women by asking questions. She had already called the cops but was still confused about what happened.

One young woman recalled how they had been horsing around in the washroom flicking water at each other. The other woman who barely stopped sobbing said, "I don't know I was running toward my room away from her after I splashed her when…I thought it was… When I turned around there were a pair of legs running behind me! Only the legs, can't make out what it was wearing!" At which point she looked up at Muskwa pointing exaggeratingly she said, "Like her nightie! It was her! It ran out the back door. There through the exit door!"

"Don't be silly! How would she do that?" the house mother replied. The memory from the past made Muskwa feel numb, the feeling cascaded over her body making her skin goose bump. She recanted from her memory the R.C.M.P and how they brought in track dogs. An hour later there were no reports of any footprints outside leaving from the exit door. Only fresh snow lay on the ground, and a house full of very scared young women.

So long ago, what really happened? Muskwa got up to pour herself another cup of coffee. She reflected on how she came across her own answer twenty-one years later. Being older had its advantages in that she had gained emotional experience and understanding of herself. Her answer to the "running legs down the corridor" happened years later, when she was slumped over a painting she had been working on. The painting would become one of the best sold out of her stock, and it's no wonder why, because on the day of realization it came through the piece she titled, "Healing Hands." Turning the time ahead, twenty-one years later with three children and a husband living on a farm, she had time in her life to pursue her passion…she painted while her kids were at school.

The demon of a memory began to surface while she was painting, and she remembered becoming angry. Anger was the only energy that could send it back into the precipices of herself. On this day she stopped and distinctly said to herself, "It's only a memory, I'm safe. It can't hurt me. Maybe if I copy what I was doing and copy the focus at the time…I might be able to unfold my understanding of what happened."

Placing her attention on her paint brush, dipping it in more blue, she recalled how it felt to sweep across the canvas. Concentrating on the pores of the linen, and the smell of the paint, she was inside of the past memory, sitting back at that desk so long ago. The desk lamp, the papers on the desk, her pencil in her hand…laughter. Feelings surfaced, outright rage…stupid little ##!!!# and then movement! A blur! Like the flash of lightening, she saw herself running after that young woman, and then spun to run out the back door!

When the realization came, it arrived quietly like a lightning bolt. She discontinued painting for a moment to absorb her answer. It felt right, but she didn't know how. And presently, right at this moment in time, she needed no witnesses. She was a witness unto herself. A fear of the dark, and fear of the unknown started to melt away with the realization of the power this held over her for so many years.

Muskwa knew and accepted that there were things in this world that might be deemed "beyond human intelligence" and this was one of her many experiences that filled an explanation. She smiled as she lifted her face to look again out of her living room window where she sat in front of her computer monitor with a profound awareness of her abilities she thought so many years ago as a curse!

Through the years in her pursuit of teachers and healing ceremonies, she found answers. One man said, *"We'll never be fully healed until we bring our broken pieces back together."* At the time it all sounded so cryptic! She was in her early thirties when people referred to her search as the "questing for a vision." The historical trauma deriving from five hundred years of assimilation, annihilation and genocide had robbed her people of the elders' their spiritual mastery, and training they received from birth. All had a unique gift;

some storytellers, medicine keepers, teleporters-those who traveled over land and water, dancers, singers, mediators, councillors and more. They shared their expertise through stories of transformation, healing circles to transmit knowledge and teachings about traditional wellness that covered psychological and physiological well-being. As one can imagine, clanships sat at the head of the table, the source of leadership to help navigate the communities. All wiped out, except for the fragments strewn across the landscape within elders who went into hiding and fell asleep.

The grandmothers referred to it as, "traditional knowledge" gone underground, which really meant it got hidden inside of her. It ran through her veins, and scientists called it DNA. With the DNA, generations of fear created by mass genocide also made up the passing of ancient knowledge. What happened to her great-grandmother, happened to her grandmother, happened to her mother, and happened to her! She quietly laughed to herself as she moved about the house cleaning dishes. What a beautiful disguise, one that every person on the earth can claim. In understanding the journey to other dimensions of existence, her ancestors (es-swi-dan in the chilcotin language) were able to go into an altered state of consciousness similar to a state of hypnosis. Through this altered state of consciousness, a breakdown of normal boundaries could be made and heightened intuition established within their psyche. This led to acute sensitivity to emotional states of others or "telepathy" (tele meaning "distant" and "pathos" for feeling or sending information from one person to another). Or the art of "telekinesis" the ability to move objects from one place to another using mental power. She thought about the intensity of the "paranoia" that occurred in her focused state, and agreed with the scientists who explained it more accurately as an increase in psychic and mental powers. In this state she had the ability to become what she focused on. When she reflected on what would happen, she could identify times when she lost all track of her body, emotions, sense of time and space. A good example was when she sat at her desk studying. At that time in her life, she was unaware of her ability to move through time and space. She thought it was a curse, she feared it! She feared herself!

Chapter Summary

The experiences Muskwa had in the unwed mother's home could now be seen in a whole new way. Her feelings had compounded through the months of confusion, lack of family support, fear, abandonment, rejection and societal segregation due to sex out of wedlock. It was like a ticking time bomb when shame contributed to "leaving her body!" In the world of healers, "leaving our body" or "out-of-body experience" or "soul travel" is an experience involving a feeling of floating outside one's body or the perception the body is separate. Most people have heard of this happening to people who died, and were later revived. For some it can be deliberately induced.

Through this chapter Muskwa shared with readers the lack of teachings, and knowledge passed down to her because of the loss of traditional knowledge that would have been handed down to her through her grandmothers. Muskwa learned about "being grounded" from an Ojibway teacher named Turtle Mother, who was good at teaching her how to spot the not so obvious. Through guidance, Muskwa became aware of her patterns and began to iden-tify them. On the evenings she could not sleep, she noticed she became bored. She remembered to relieve the boredom, she could apply a technique learned from her elder. Focusing on her chest, she counted how many times her chest went up and then down while she breathed. After a few moments, she felt herself drifting but it felt like she was awake, her eyelids were closed. Oh! And that strange feeling; paranoia flooded her being. She noted this strange feeling occurred during the day, sometimes when she was uneasy with the person she was with, or in a group of people. Then it came, someone tapped her on the shoulder. Instead of being frightened, she focused on who or what happened. Within in a split second she caught a fleeting image! It was her, as she arose above her body, and tapped herself! It was her! Muskwa awoke right at the moment of the tap! She had been scaring herself! After realizing her gifted capacity to leave her body, she no longer experienced hauntings in her space. *The years of pokes, and taps when she was a child was her spirit self-attempting to prove she could leave her body!*

Exercise

Practice becoming "present" to enable "focus" and "grounding". Does your movement change when you are anxious? If so how? What about tasks? Do you do comb your hair a certain way? Why? When you go to bed at night become aware of how you feel, what triggered the feelings and the amount of energy within you. To have a good night's sleep, you will need energy to sleep! Like Muskwa, notice the feelings about darkness and light. After doing the exercise for a few nights, why not try focusing on your breathing? Focus on your chest rising and falling, sometimes it's all you need to drift off and have the best night's sleep. How does it feel? Keep a journal and record your thoughts each day. It's through your writing you will notice a gentle but subtle shift in your perceptions. You will notice day-to-day things when you actively practice being "in the moment," or "in presence," and it will provide new awareness's for you.

THREE

GOD IN ADDICTION?

Dawn Star

D riving down the road, window rolled down, wind in her hair and rocking to Metallica's "Whisky in a Jar," the young elder drove into the mall's parking lot. She loved the music of the 60's. Just before she was preparing to turn the car off, an old tune from CCR's (Creedance Clearwater) "Bad Moon Rising," sounded loudly from her stereo. As she listened to the tunes belt out into the space of her car, she could see her late brother's face smiling back at her. Like the setting of the "Dawn Star" upon the horizon, he was just like the star that plunged into the darkness below the skyline. Her late brother came into his physical life a wanderer and exited in the evanescence of its path.

Muskwa's eyes affixed on the rear view mirror as she thought about a dream she had about her late brother. In the dream she recalled how she entered the forest at nightfall. Her breathing shallowed as she went down a hill. When she moved slowly to a clearing she noted the glow from kerosene lamps had filled the space. She found herself by a fire, and in this place a strange white noise echoed from the colors she saw. She felt him come closer to her, and he said, "What are you doing here? You have to leave now!" Muskwa took in the surrounding area and memorized it so that she could bring it back to waking with her. The place resembled a treatment center for souls. She replied, "I wanted to see you. I love you." Before she could say anymore, he showed her upwards her exit out. An energy enveloped her and guided her to the path. Her breathing became labored, the walk up the hill was so steep she remembered! She recalled how she gasped for air when she awoke, his face was vividly upon her mind's eye. As she finished thinking about her dream, she noticed other vehicles pulling up beside hers.

When she was one and a half years old, her mother brought him home from the hospital. A blurred image of her sitting behind a couch, and her screaming at the top of her lungs, "No! I don't want a baby brother! Take it back!" The face of the babysitter and her mother laughing at her while they tried to coax her from behind the couch. At that tender age she knew baby brother was here to stay!

Credence Clearwater's bad moon began to fade as it ended, and Muskwa locked her car door. As she walked towards the mall's entrance her memories of her late brother continued to flood in. As children growing up together, her parents demanded she look after her little brother. Where ever she went—take your brother! With no parental tools, she didn't know how to protect him from schoolyard bullying or how to prevent fights. She recanted the times she jumped in to help, only to discover later her brother was tagged as a "weeny" or "weakling" which subjected him to more bullying. Her brother Twin Eagle had a soft heart and no matter what he did, he couldn't hit someone else. Muskwa's father would drone on about "getting the fists up and taking it like a man," no conciliation to the number of times he came home with black eyes, bruises or scratches because he was in a fight with a school yard bully.

Muskwa's attention reverted back to her grocery shopping; she dug into her purse for her wallet as she approached the till. The cashier digitally entered the amount owing as Muskwa prepared to insert her debit card. As she gathered her bagged groceries, she returned to the memory of her late brother. She remembered asking her mother why there was only one baby photo?

When Twin Eagle came into this world, she remembered how nurturing and loving her mother had been. A shift in her mother's behavior began when Twin Eagle was four and spankings became a weird type of competition for Two Eagle. When Red Tree broke the wooden spoons on his bottom, Two Eagle would look up at her and laugh. She'd rush for her hair brush and "wham!" right across his rear end! Nothing seemed to affect him, and in the end he pretended to cry. Muskwa intuited there was something wrong with her brother's reaction. She remembered begging her brother not to push their mother so they both wouldn't get it. *"It would have been nice for her father to get out of bed and save them,"* she thought. Her father worked night shifts, and spent the day sleeping so they hardly ever saw their dad. When they did, he was running about while Red Tree packed his lunch bag with sandwiches and coffee.

The projection of anger became an all too familiar behavior in her household. One time her brother had shared with the neighbor how their mother needed to take pills. They were never to talk to the neighbors about anything! A spanking followed, and there were times when bruises were left.

Time had a funny way of healing wounds. Before she was ten years old she recalled her mother leaving and how empty the house felt. Her father said her mother was drinking in the bars and refused to come home. In a desperate attempt to bring her back to raise her children, her father phoned the bar. *"Please, can't you put her on the black list you have behind the counter? You know that little black book?"* he pleaded. *"Sir, we don't do that anymore. That was so long ago!"* said the bartender's voice on the other end of the phone. Back in the 1950's a man could put his wife, mother, or sister's name in a black book at the bars and to be banned forever. Her mother disappeared a few more times, until the day she never came back and it was followed up with "divorce papers."

Time rolled by and they arrived into their early teens. She remembered her brother's anger and defiance but it was blurred by her own rebellion. It wasn't long when they found a way to get bootlegged liquor, "oh, how sweet it was!" she thought to herself. Most refer to it as liquid courage,as it helped the feeling of "smallness" and "inadequacy" disappear. It was a time when an inflated sense of popularity emerged; and overgrown arrogance that wanted to test everyone.

Muskwa was nudged back to the present as she arrived back home. Unloading the groceries with the sun on her face, she felt honored by the presence of life. Gratitude filled her heart. What did the past matter? As she reflected, it became important to capture the lessons from this time in her life. If she were asked to summarize her current, life what would she say?

Opening the door, the sunlight poured into her kitchen as she started to unpack the groceries and place them into her cupboards. Reflecting back to her current question she thought, "God in addiction?" To her it made perfect sense, because in her early teens both she and her brother drank because it started out as fun.

As a naïve teen, when the alcohol went down, all sense of responsibility, lack of popularity or even that of unacceptance created by peer pressure, disappeared. Here they didn't think about being children from the other side of the tracks, or wagon burners, or Indians. All they had to do was find a bootlegger to revisit the warmth of hard liquor and all the worries and frustrations peeled away.

Liquor had brought a false sense of security, feelings of comfort that increased over time, and she recalled the urge to drink increased. Whether in physical pain, or emotional/mental rejection, abandonment or verbal abuse, the alcohol numbed her senses and acted as a painkiller to get through her own self-loathing. Within the confines of drunkenness, she found courage, and here she could act out a part—she could commune with spirit. It felt like a communion with god, and for a short time in her life it was a lifestyle that all-consumed her body, mind and spirit.

Eventually, with near-miss car accidents, and the run of abusive relationships, she recalled giving it all up for her children. Motherhood was her everything, as contact with her brother became distanced when he moved away. Years unfolded, some calls she received from him, and then more years illusively passed by. As her children grew into adults moving out on their own, there was with little contact with her brother. Last she recalled, he was living with their father, and working.

Then that one day as she opened her inbox, there sat an email from a relative it read:

> *"Muskwa, I hope this letter finds you and your family in good health. I have some sad news to pass along. Your brother Two Eagles has passed away. Your family has been trying to get a hold of you by phone with no success; I've tried a couple of numbers and didn't get an answer. Please call me when you can. May the great spirit watch over you all."*

The unimaginable happened, a time of dread that most families can't conceive, and for Muskwa it was the loss of her brother. She lifted her head as she moved through her house. She looked at the red binder on the shelf, went to it and pulled it out. Within it contained old letters she never received from Two Eagle. Aside from a few binders, the papers were all that was left from him.

She thought about him, and what he would say to others from the spirit world, and what he would want her to say to others about "addiction." She read somewhere that human weakness was in the effects of "feel good" opiates, and how the human brain could release its own chemicals during pleasure when shopping, eating, clothing, sex, alcohol and so forth. Her teachers said, "If its consumption is above moderate, using it becomes an addiction." The cravings blurred boundaries, and values of self-worth declined through frequent use by the individual. She recognized how her own past addictive cycle had crossed over from the normalcy of behavior into damaging friendships or other connections she had at the time.

She marveled at the three words "god in addiction." During relief found in the euphoria created by the drunken or drugged stupor she elicited during those days—she made a choice! She chose to break the cycle! Her late brother remained in the addiction—extinguishing any connection to her, or her children ever getting to know him outside of the alcohol as a brother or uncle involved in family outings, talks or walks. The events of hunting, or creation of memories to build healthy relationships didn't happen.

Prior to his death, Two Eagles ended up in jail for several impaired driving charges and he was forced to clean up. Two letters and one journal entry from treatment were found and are what remained of his legacy. Muskwa's only inheritance and memory of him was now held in a red binder. It read:

HUDTA LAKE CORRECTIONAL CENTRE

Letter

Hi Muskwa,
The existence of a higher power to my life seems to have always been there but always had been drowned out from all the booze. All and all, I think today is the first day of the rest of my life. Red Tree and Uncle are coming to pick me up I think. I'm sure looking forward to seeing them. It'll be good to see family again. We're having a group meeting right now and I'm writing you a letter. Two things at one time and I am good. Oh well. We're talking about what we want out of a sponsor. It'll be my turn in about 2 seconds. Well, I told them what I wanted out of a sponsor, and basically repeated what everyone else wants out of a sponsor. I'll be going out that way sometime soon, for I want to pay my respects to our grandmother. Maybe you can accompany me? So many things I never did and wanted to do be closer to her. I'm going to write a letter to her, it's the only thing I can do to justify my feelings; that, and pay my respects. (Grandmother had passed away while he was in jail.) I'll be on parole until October and just knowing that scares me, getting back into my own way of life again scares me but I have an even mind to set things into motion. So with that I'll leave you now. Say hi to your kids and hubby for me and I'll see you when I see you. Love your brother.

Letter #2

Hi Muskwa!

I received your letter and I thank you for the words from the heart. It's interesting to understand about how I was able to comprehend what you said. Seven months ago I would have ignored the words and wouldn't have seen or felt the words from your heart. Well, this will be my last letter you will receive from me in this place, as I'm out of here Thursday 20th*. That gives me three more days here. I'll be back in home staying with our father until I get a little bit ahead, money wise. I'll be going back to work sometime in May so everything seems on the up and up. I was just thinking the other day, in this program we have steps to follow in AA and I finished step 8. When I was finished step 5, I believe I had a spiritual awakening. It said, "I admitted to God, to ourselves and another human being the exact nature of our wrong." I did the step with father Ivan at his place and really opened up to him and the heavy burden was lifted. All of a sudden there was more space to move around, and I finally found serenity. All my fears had been removed. I really believe after I told someone about the ugliness that lived inside of me it made room for my real emotions. I am back to being the person I always was, real.*

The last entries of Twin Eagle's treatment he wrote about his addiction:

"When I am powerless to the chemicals placed in my life, the types of jeopardy I faced were a result of three key factors. I noticed my physical well-being deteriorated, once a man weighing a little over 140 lbs at the age of 30, plummeted to

100 to 110 lbs. I could barely look in the mirror, I hated the image looking back! His head was so big! And collar bones jutted out from underneath the t-shirt! Secondly, I noticed my judgment placed people in danger. When I was scared or mad I wanted to drive, it didn't matter if I had a few drinks-who would know? Then there was the part where I let anyone drive my vehicle while they were drinking too. I lost self-respect because of my chemical usage, in this case alcohol. I couldn't have a relationship for very long. After a while it didn't matter what I looked like, I had given up personal care and who gives a crap what others think about me anyway? If there was a problem, I didn't know how to deal with it because I didn't stay long enough to be responsible. Money was for drinking, so I was always in the poor house. I had no self-respect, I continually put myself down because I hated myself. I realize through my treatment process that the behavior my family objected to the most was that I was always unhappy. I had a "I don't give a damn" attitude, and had to continue drinking when everyone else was done. When it came to controlling my drinking, I knew better than to drink at work. I also knew that if I avoided relatives I could stay sober, and I could fill my time doing other things with my spouse. I want to share with you a thought about an experience that demonstrates my powerlessness. After I had four car accidents, it hit me one day while I was driving. I had to stop the car. A feeling of desperation overcame me, I was shaking and someway I was scared to even go on driving. I remembered every one of those accidents clear as day, what a fool I was! It was a very bad awakening. Now, the five examples of powerlessness (loss of control) that have affected my life.

1   *I had just enough money but bought alcohol instead. Or had a food voucher and sold it for half the price just enough for a bottle of wine.*

2   *Bumming money off the street corner as a desperate attempt to get a bottle.*

3   *Have maybe two dollars and smiling I'd say, "it's a start!" then I would go bumming around.*

4   *Go to another town in the car with little or not enough gas to make it there because we had to have booze for the trip.*

5   *Pawning off half the household for more but it was never enough.*

I think there are other attributes like physical abuse that happened to me or others as a result of my chemical usage. I obtained scars on my face after a girlfriend during an argument smashed a beer bottle into my face. The ninety stitches to my face took forever to heal. The same girlfriend slashed her wrist one night, as the ambulance rushed to our place we held her wrist and upper arm together. What a mess, she went straight up with the tip of the fish knife from her wrist upwards. I've had my face, and body slammed to whatever it was a number of times. I'd awake in a pool of blood, get up and go into the house to fix it all back up. I don't think I ever won any of the fights. My current physical condition (heart-liver?) I have bad teeth, noticeable face scars, a bad liver and an ulcer. Here I get to answer what I think the difference between admittance and acceptance of my problem is. I'm 31 years old, and I can tell you that when I set these goals they only worked for a very short time. I did realize that I had to quit setting standards so high for myself.

Chapter Summary

Muskwa realized as a child she didn't have adequate tools to parent her brother, and it was never her job to be given the responsibility to raise her brother. In her healing process, Muskwa let go of the guilt around being "irresponsible in protecting her brother." You see, she wasn't responsible for his choices. Twin Eagle had grown into adulthood and was answerable to the same choices.

Exercise – Saying Goodbye

Step 1: In your journal, take the time to reflect on one or more important things you want to let go of and for each one, try to replace them with things you could do instead.

Step 2: Think about the people who like or love you, as it will make it easier to say goodbye to a person, place or thing that isn't good for you.

Step 3: Find a confidant, someone you know, like and trust, and who you can openly share your thoughts with once a week.

Step 4: Keep track of your progress by writing in your journal every day.

FOUR

DIRTY 30'S FATHER

Father

L ike a big old bear, Muskwa stretched her arms above her and loudly yawned as the first light filtered through her curtains. She was thankful for the warmth of lessons from her past elders who held high regard for the sun's energies. Shifting herself, she got up to find her coffee maker's already perked black gold—such gratitude for mother earth's gift this fine morning.

If there was one thing Muskwa learned in her life's journey, it was her gratitude for all the things before her. Her eyes shifted towards the window, a beautiful memory about a ceremony her Cree/Ojibway extended family called the "Sundance" flooded back to her. It was like she could smell the cedar burning inside the lodge, hear the whistles as they blew. The vision gave her admiration; her love floated towards the community of men who held the ceremony.

Such respect and high regard for "grandfather sun" and its teaching for the men to align with it to heal themselves. She recalled a story told to her about the Sundance Lodge. When creator made humans, it made man and then it made another who would bring life into this world. For the Sioux, "Wiyan" (Wee yan) translated as *"little creator,"* described the woman in their language. At the time she heard the translation, Muskwa fell deeper in love with cultural languages. The lilt of the First Nation language, and the renditions of stories and lessons, continued to hold its mystery for her. In the lesson of the sun, she recalled how Creator aligned the woman's' energy with a twenty-eight-day cycle, and then combined it with the moon. The alliance with the moon would help women heal, nurture her babies, heighten her intuition, and give ease to her heart when there were difficulties. With much consideration, creator gave men the gift of the Sundance ceremony to help them cleanse, and to also heal physically, but in a different way. Within his healing rite, a man could offer his body, surrender his mind, and connect with his spirit by handing himself to the creator when he danced with the sun—a men's ceremony. It was stressed to women *"what happens in the men's lodge, stays in the men's lodge. Women had their teachings, and needed to focus upon them."* Muskwa noted women and men had their own circles for healing. From her recollection, men did not run women's lodges, nor the women run men's ceremonies unless it had been unveiled to an individual through a teacher. To her understanding, through historical genocide, assimilation and acculturation perpetuated upon cultural people; all cultures including Aboriginal communities lost their teaching foundations for both men and women. Teachings had become blurred, personal boundaries disappeared along with "self-respect," and "respect of others."

It took her years to understand the term "respect men" because she had not done her healing enough to grasp the messages. Then one day, an awareness came to her right out of the blue. When she left home, letter writing was reciprocal for both her and her father. She recalled his responses were carefully penned with cursive writing on airline paper. It meant so much to her that she saved them, and they now sat in that "red binder" on the shelf. Muskwa's story of her father contained words that described him as, "out there, not present or a weird thinker." She received a few stories about his growing up years but very little in terms of family origin.

Muskwa couldn't recall her father's sisters because he hardly talked about his family structure. She had limited information to validate how her father grew up, and her father Big Rock Man didn't fully contribute his life story. What stood out for her was his overprotective parenting, fear and lack of family connections. Her childhood experience said, "He didn't like people," and he reaffirmed the lack of faith in humanity by saying things like "neighbors like to talk filth!" He didn't seem to share an awareness around "why he didn't like people." In light of her thoughts, her father was a night watchman for a big company and this fascinated her.

Throughout his life, her father constantly battled a type of schizophrenic arch-nemesis: best described as hallucinations with visual and/or auditory illusions he responded aloud to.

That moment of awareness presented itself to her when she separated her father from his "*behaviour.*" She recalled various times when he shouted, "those dirty minded men, those dirty dirty neighbors! The filth!" Yet, other times he was present emotionally and mentally. She couldn't say he was prone to doing it *all the time.* The truth was there were times he was a really loving person. She had to agree, some of his responses were confusing, especially when he went about saying things like, "Dirt poor," "Never lie," "Never steal! They'll throw away the key!" "They'll lock you up in sing sing!" Oh, those invisible talking voices he had, and she had become accustomed to while growing up. The pieces of the puzzle started to come together for her when a family member shared her father's past and she was able to tie it to his term "sing sing."

As Muskwa recanted the story told to her by a relative, she was brought into the year 1952. She saw a man around nineteen years old playing music in his 1946 Plymouth Special. Another vehicle pulled up behind the Plymouth and parked quietly while the man snapped his fingers to his favorite tune. It was Big Rock Man enjoying the comfort of his car, and it was night fall and the tunes were belting out from the radio. Suddenly his behavior changed from celebratory to that of paranoia, he hears whispers, talking through the radio again? She saw her father in the time zone of the past trying hard not to react. The voices said horrible things about him! "Doggon it! Where is it coming from?" She imagined him saying.

Big Rock Man reeled to look through his side mirrors where he saw a car, lights on and realized it might not be the radio after all! There were a couple of people talking about him. He would straighten this matter out! In his youthful cockiness, Big Rock Man got out of his Plymouth and stormed to the car behind him all the while ranting obscenities. He was quickly arrested by the men who turned out to be policemen. Does the story end there? She thought about "sing sing" and what would happen to a man hearing voices in 1952. From what she remembered being told, Big Rock Man was taken to a local hospital, where he was hospitalized for a month.

Muskwa shifted in her seat uncomfortably, "a person really doesn't know the truth about another's story until they hear the rest of the story." She reflected deeper, like a witness in the time warp she watched her father being hauled into the hospital. So horrible! What was the reason for treating him like he was dangerous? She saw the sign of the times; there had been advancements in medicine to treat people who exhibited psychosis or mental disorders exhibited by the loss of reality either through irrational type thinking, projected emotional responses or unwarranted physical reactions. Suddenly Muskwa was brought back to reality, and she jumped up to look in the "red binder" for the research she had found on shock therapy. She thumbed through the various pages and quickly came across it. Muskwa read:

Shock therapy had become a popular treatment in this time and it was administered by a "*white coated psychiatric specialist*" who gained a reputation as being a "*witch doctor*" who would scare out, shake out, or exorcize the demons or devils that caused the person to behave in a deplorable way. The cure for this illness was to bring about the quiet and submissiveness from the patient.

> "*The patient is put through a crucifixion of such torment as one would wish to spare the lowliest animal.*"
>
> —FRANK, 2005

The awareness filtered into her consciousness, and recalled when she was a child her dad slept during the day because he worked as a night foreman. Today, she marveled in his choices because not only did he work by himself away from people, but he escaped questioning about his mental stability and made sure he was safe from the risk of being discovered by his biggest fear, the "white coats." His auditory and visual delusions didn't immobilize his ability to look after himself, or prevent him from raising his children.

Her father "Big Rock Man" never talked about himself. He was constant in his extreme expression and paranoia of the Doukhobor's or Hutterites. He feared they would discover he said something and come after him. His immediate response was to shut the conversation down! In a pursuit of getting to know her father, Muskwa remembered the incredible amount of persistence she applied when asking him questions. If one question didn't bring about a conversation, she waited and tried again. *"Some days are diamonds, others were like pennies,"* she had written in one of her journals to describe the pursuit of her father's history and his life experiences. One memory he shared with her contained a caravan of Indians arriving at her dad's grandfather's door step. Her father recalled, *"You didn't want to ignore them! Boy, they were poor and starving to death those poor buggers. So desperate were they! There were rumors, warning us to feed them because they would kill you just for something to eat. They came in wagons; you know the kind horses pull. My grandfather fed them what they had, and the Indians left quietly. That's all you had to do! But some didn't see it that way,"* he said. It seemed surreal to Muskwa that her father didn't see her brown skin, or recognise his ex-wife as Aboriginal? And the term he used "Indian" was likened to a separate people in his story.

Her prodding for more information resulted in him sharing family lineage. He said to her, *"Yep, we're Ukrainian—my mother's name was so long you couldn't say it. She passed away when I was ten years old. My father was Hungarian."* Muskwa reveled in the generational details. She had not known her father's lineage until he shared it with her. At the time she recalled being in late thirties! There was still the mystery of her maiden name and its origin being traced back to Scotland.

Her father's upbringing appeared to be very mysterious, as he only talked about a small school house and having to work by the time he was in grade seven. She recalled times when a thunder storm would set off her father's panic, all curtains were shut to cover the windows. No one could be on the telephone, or in the bathtub. In her recollection a towel or blanket was used to cover the mirrors to prevent lightening from striking it.

Muskwa finished sipping on her first cup of morning coffee, and went for her second cup. It was time for her to make breakfast; her father always had minced garlic in everything. She thought about how she smelled like garlic when she went to school and figured maybe it was the reason why she wasn't so popular. After her mother left her father, he was left to cook for a little while. He taught her how to cook with sauerkraut, garlic and onions, all his favorites. He swore the garlic was a cure all for everything.

Is it a wonder why she didn't trust physicians? One time when she was around eleven years old, she recanted her father sharing what his doctor said, *It looks as if you have mouth cancer. We will need to run a biopsy and some tests.* To which she recalled her father sharing with her, *"No damn way!"* He then showed her his mouth, so white inside like a piece of paper. She was a child then and didn't know what it meant to have cancer. Soon their diet was chock full of raw garlic in everything! In the mashed potato pot it provided such a wonderful taste! Garlic, it was cooked, steamed and fried in all of their foods. "How long did this go on?" she thought to herself. He went to another appointment and the doctor asked, *"How did you do that?"* His response, *"You wouldn't believe me if I told you."* After the prognosis, there was no more discussion about cancer.

In part, to understand her dad's generation with very little to go on, Muskwa recreated his story by collecting information from history books, and her interest gave way to studying history in her university courses. There on her bookshelf sat a binder with lessons from first European contact, photo copied research on the "Great Depression." She reached up again and brought the black three-inch binder down to view its contents. As Muskwa flipped a couple of pages, she noted her scrawled notes on her father's era:

It was called the "Great Depression" because the stock market crash of 1929 causing a series of events that rippled through Canada. Likened to the effects of skipping a pebble over the water, the effects created one condition – no work, then another – no food, and then its formation into one huge societal wave of poverty. Millions of Canadian people were unemployed, hungry and homeless due to fallen wheat prices and other farm products that could no longer be sold. Poverty was compounded further by a crippling Prairies drought and it triggered welfare, and food stamps. From 1929 to around 1933 there were no changes in the economy, and when Muskwa's dad was conceived, his mother was probably more than malnourished. Women during this time were not only mothers but also found work as "cleaning women" or in "factory jobs." Long hours were spent toiling at work. As a farmer's wife, Muskwa saw her grandmother without modern conveniences such as water and electricity. This meant packing water and splitting wood to keep the house warm. Her dad's mother experienced the impending fear of poverty, she coped with stress, and received a mere pittance for her daily work. Sometimes when things were really tight, women like her grandmother exchanged their labour for product. That meant washing floors or any other physical labour during her pregnancy to help put food on the table.

While listening to a documentary a few months ago, Muskwa heard how poverty had played into the DNA of the WWII unborn children. Pregnant mothers faced incredible stressors, hunger and malnourishment. It wasn't uncommon for her to have stillbirths or deliver a sick child into the world. Scientists discovered children of this era arriving into their adult years faced mental and emotional disorders or psychosis when the impending nature of poverty was no longer a concern. Their findings were related to the effects upon an unborn child in the womb when the mother was malnourished due to the lack of nutrients created by starvation.

With this knowledge, Muskwa put the pieces of the puzzle together to understand her father. Growing up with a father who had a "scarcity mindset" and lack of "self-value," Muskwa started to understand her belief systems were not all her own. She could now separate the "scarcity mindset beating" her father imposed upon her with different awareness's and how its attributes affected her life. She also knew she *had the highest level of awareness in her relationship with her father. Becoming more aware had placed her in a leadership role in the relationship and a responsibility to now let go of her past interpretation of her father's illness."*

She saw her father in a whole new light – he was a warrior, a legend in his own right; someone who survived society's earlier interpretation, diagnosis and treatment of what it deemed mentally ill patients.

Chapter Summary & Exercise

Break Through The Barrier Exercise

Be willing to see both sides of the story. In this exercise you choose to exercise first to forgive yourself, then forgiveness of the person of your inquiry or forgiveness to those around you. Forgiveness is for those who want to play "full out." Forgiveness begins with the process of unraveling the part that condemns others with a paragraph that begins with, *"they always do this to me. It always happens to me…"* The process seeks to "blame others" rather than to take ownership. It's really about fear, and there comes a time when the belief *"no longer serves us."* Forgiveness will call upon you to separate the beating from the behavior. You don't need to know the other's full story or their intentions. To succeed, agree that you don't understand their true intentions or behavior (letting go of our story) to separate beating from the behavior with a question that follows, "do they always do that?" Or can you narrow it down to a few incidences?

Like Muskwa, is there something you can do to help you understand what was taking place in the other person's life history? Some families have rich history, photos, albums, paper work, documentation, and other sources for clues. Other families had very little written history but provided stories as fragments and pieces to a bigger picture.

Changing a programmed belief system will take work. The longer it has been in our lives, expect time for it to change by consistently reprogramming through the writing of affirmations and placing them where your eyes will frequently rest upon them. Muskwa likes to write on her bathroom or dressing mirror. Here's one you can use to help get you started. *"I release and forgive you and I now enter my life whole."*

If you can't get through this exercise practice "passing it to SPIRIT" in your prayers. Remember when Creator or God dreamed, it dreamed YOU.

FIVE

WITCH DOCTOR

Grandmother Within

I n the early morning hours Muskwa rolled over in bed. She adjusted her pillows, pounded them and moved them around. Her ankles ached and her shoulder blade muscles pounded. She arose from her bed to put 'Indian tea' on the stove to heat up. Within a few minutes she poured the heated liquid into her cup.

She sat down looking out the big bay window in her living room. Through the spruce tree limbs, she watched as daylight emerged, a hint of grey within the morning light and it captured her eyes. Sipping the hot tea, the essence of the earth's elixirs tantalized her taste buds, the beverage's natural taste, its healing blends comprised of a concoction of roots, leaves and bark she collected from the bush. A natural remedy for arthritis an elder taught her many years ago. Slowly sipping the tea, she remembered a black acrid liquid her grandmother gave to her when she was a child.

As she continued to sip the Indian tea she recalled the reoccur-ring tonsillitis infections that sent her home from school frequently when she was seven years old. The flu-like symptoms brought on high fever, swollen neck glands, and some nasty infections that created breathing problems and the ability to swallow solid foods. She spent so much time sick that Muskwa failed her first grade of school. Her father didn't like doctors and Muskwa had little memory of seeing one until she was ten years old. Her father finally decided a medical diagnosis of her ongoing sickness was necessary. Their family doctor strongly recommending a tonsillectomy and adenoidectomy to correct the problem when she was ten years old. Afterwards, her health improved dramatically.

Prior to the removal of her tonsils, she recollected a summer's trip to her mother's homeland. It was a memorable time for her because the trip had taken them on a long drive into the bush on gravel roads to her mother's parent's home. Bush life was so differ-ent, as it didn't provide running water from the tap, or lights run by electricity. When she walked into her grandparent's cabin for the very first time she was greeted by so many aunts, uncles and cousins' smiling faces. During that visit she would grow fond of her grandfather because he had horses. He also had the gift of teasing, and the moment she cherished the most was when he placed her right behind him, and her brother behind her on the saddle to go for a ride!

Muskwa sat smiling smugly while she drank her tea and allowed the images and voices of the past flood into her memory. As her grandfather rode down the dirt pathway, her brother complained he was scared he was going to slide off the tail of the horse. Grandfather laughed, "Hold on then!" He gently kicked the horse's side and off the trio galloped, riding full-speed. Muskwa heard the squeals and yells from her childhood past. Then the splash of water as he steered the horse into the lake! Her grandfather laughed and teased. "Are we there yet?" Twin Eagle said in a voice of loud protest. Then they were off to the cabin in a full gallop, Twin Eagle holding on tight.

Muskwa's smile held as she tipped the cup of tea to her mouth and finished the last swallow. During this visit she fell sick, her throat swollen and once again she was in bed with a fever. She vaguely recalled the adults who talked about how far it was to drive to a hospital, and her mother's concern for her rising fever. Then her grandmother sat beside her on the bed, with her mother Red Tree standing closely who said, *"Granny is going to take the sickness away and make you feel better ok?"* Nodding in agreement, her grandmother held her head; it felt good because her hands were cool.

The next day she was up free from the fever and swollen neck. She was running around like nothing had happened. Her mother Red Tree said, "I told you that you'd get better!" as Muskwa ran outside. The visit faded from her memory. It was the first and last time she would hear the laughter of her grandfather again.

Muskwa marvelled at her grandmother's healing abilities recognized today as "Reiki" or "Hands of Light" techniques to move stagnate energies with gentle facilitations to trigger the flow within the human body. As a child not wanting to be sick, she didn't pay too much to what the adults were doing in their world. All she wanted to do as a child was to be healthy and return to her childhood activities. After her grandfather passed away, in the month of July she would visit her mother's homeland and the tonsillitis returned. When she woke up in the morning, Muskwa experienced the usual swelling and sore throat. Her grandmother led her to the outskirts of the camp, made her sit down and wait while she went into the bush. Muskwa distinctly recalled becoming restless; it seemed like she had waited a long time when her grandmother emerged from the bush carrying a handful of tree boughs from the bush. Quietly

Muskwa had watched her grandmother make a hot drink over a fire she had built. Soon a metal cup about one quarter full with an ebony black liquid mixture was passed to her. In broken English her grandmother said, "Drink it," motioning for her to drink the tea. Muskwa wrinkled her nose. Her grandmother pushed the cup closer to Muskwa and demanded a little more firmly for her to drink the tea. There didn't seem to be any way out of drinking the tea. It looked horrible so it must be horrible! She recalled pinching her nose and gulping the tea down. It was bitter! The next day, her throat was better! The summer came and went, and Muskwa didn't see her grandmother again until she had her own children.

Muskwa came back from the memory as she was moving around the house. Her aching almost gone when she thought about a man who came into her life who was called a "medicine man," a term she was unfamiliar with. At first meeting, she didn't pay too much attention to him when he came to visit staff at her work site. Her first impression of him was that he was "peculiar"; he wore his long black hair in braids, and he had on a pair of beaded moccasins.

During one of his visits he came to see her and asked her, "Where did her family come from?" She told him about the mountains, and he asked about her family which she supposed led to talking about her grandmother. *"Yeah, some say she's a witch doctor,"* she said. She recalled his response, *"The correct term for her is medicine woman. Witch Doctor is the term given to your grandmother's abilities by the churches who banned the practice of healing."* The response triggered confusion and a need to know more about the practice of healing. She had not understood how her grandmother healed her, nor did she grasp the abilities needed to take illness away. Like a moth takes to light, Muskwa remembered going to most of his workshops on natural healing. She attended feasts and ceremonies over a period of five years to understand the pieces of the puzzle. As more questions were answered, more questions surfaced about her people's original way of life. Learning about traditional healing by means of earth awareness, natural wellness and health made her feel at home. She recalled her thirst to learn more, to understand how her family lived centuries ago off the land and how alive she felt upon each lesson learned!

While she moved about the house, she became restless thinking about the past, old ways and the bush. The sound of the morning was filled with the atmosphere of noise coming from electrical household appliances. The buzzing was driving her crazy, and she couldn't relax! She yearned for quiet, the solace of the land, and its need registered strongly in her senses when she found herself packing her camping equipment.

Muskwa proceeded down the gravel road in her car. Straight out of the blue, she had decided enough is enough of the city. The concrete jungle with its own busyness of traffic, people in a rush, and the constant electrical hum was assistance in her quick decision. She knew when it was time to return to nature, and it was when her sleep patterns consisted of endless tossing and turning.

After a few hours of driving, she randomly chose a gravel side road out of the city, and drove to find a camping spot. She found one in no time. Muskwa liked trips like these, no plan, just a random selection of turns to mark a destination. She decided to pitch her tent quickly before she set out to enjoy her afternoon. It wasn't long before she headed out for her walk. Now surrounded by the green pine trees, wild grasses, butterflies, flying insects, flowers and earth smells, she started to feel more relaxed. The stress rolled off her shoulders, and a feeling of calm entered her being. As she walked, the plants called upon her memory of their individual properties. She sighted Labrador tea, its leaves dark green, its smell of musk reminiscent of her childhood. Nearby young shoots of fireweed grew, its root used for the flu. Across from it underneath the lodge pole pines, a moss used for addictions, and another the elderly women claimed healed tuberculosis. Muskwa imagined what it would have been like for her ancestors who lived off the land. She pictured her own footsteps following her ancestors' as they picked Labrador tea leaves and placed them in spruce root baskets. Traveling back to the year 1870, she might have heard her great-grandmother say, *"Drink it for stomach problems."* Like her ancestors, the earth's plants, trees, roots, leaves, seeds, berries, flowers and bark, held endless healing possibilities.

Muskwa remembered a story her mother Red Tree shared with her about her grandmother named "Wild Sunflower," while her eyes took in the flora fauna of the borealis forest on her walk.

"Wild Sunflower was sixteen years old when she got really sick. There she laid by the fire of the outdoor camp. She hardly moved all day, and she had a hard time breathing. She said her chest felt heavy. Nightfall came quickly and her mother "Wolf" motioned her daughter Wild Sunflower to lay on her back. The great-grandmother leaned over Wild Sunflower and tapped her chest to awaken her. Wolf opened her eyes and in recognition nodded to her mother to proceed. Wild Sunflower kneeled, then placed her mouth upon her daughter's chest. She stayed in this knelt over position for a few minutes. When she came up she pointed to her mouth, then gestured to the fire. In the firelight Wild Sunflower saw Wolf blow a black fluid into the fire. Wildflower recalled her mother swooping over her chest one more time to draw the sickness out of her chest, blowing it into the fire. The next day I wasn't sick anymore."

The images of the past held her grandmothers' so vividly. The dancing firelight, shadows cast upon the images. As they faded, Muskwa reverted to the present. Her grandmother Wild Sunflower didn't know what type of illness she had back then. With a bit of research Muskwa discovered her grandmother's symptoms illustrated tuberculosis (TB), a hallmark illness in history for Aboriginal people. In 1930 documentations from provincial archives recorded thousands of Aboriginal children and adults who were placed in Canadian infirmaries for TB who never recovered. Whether her grandmother had TB or the flu, the art of traditional healing was still being practiced despite the ban of spiritual practices by the government Indian Act until 1954. Muskwa recalled seeing dandelion that had grown through a cement walkway. A weed to be exterminated by some, a powerful healing derivative to others. Like the dandelion, the Aboriginal practices of the "witch doctor" retained their knowledge despite the assimilation.

She had finished her walk through the bush and was building a fire now. As she applied the lavender and tea tree oils to her skin to keep the mosquitoes off, the smell of the smoke drifted in her face. There were so many stories told by an evening camp fire, only to be told at night because each story called in ancestral spirits. It was important not to tell them in the day as the night spirits couldn't find their way in the daylight. The loud crackling of the fire brought Muskwa back to the present. She stoked the fire she built and gathered more dry twigs and branches from the land. She returned to her thinking about "witch doctor." Hearing its correction "medicine woman" had created a pivotal time in her life.

Underneath the words "witch doctor" was a practice of assimilation and genocide of her people she was unaware of because of her upbringing off-reserve. Muskwa didn't know what to think when she heard of Canadian families who never heard about residential schooling, or about the genocide inflicted on a people through the "Indian Act." She understood how censorship in T.V. and newspapers before its release could cover up the incidents. Media reported successes in education of Indian children, showing only smiles and laughter of happy children within the residential school system. Yet the insidiousness of abuses that occurred behind closed doors became the hallmark of its dark secrecy to the world.

She thought about the arrival of the Europeans and the destruction of Aboriginal communities and their matriarchal societies, a place where women were enamoured for creating life. How the Sioux communities knew woman as 'wiyan' (wee-yan) meaning "little creator," one who was chosen besides God to create life. How women held prestigious positions such as healing, council, leadership, guidance, psychology, pharmacy, archeology, astronomy and more. Women were consulted by the men when decisions needed resolution, and in oral storytelling. She was also positioned to create the clan structure in the Mohawk long house system to help men identify and give organization to their roles in the community. Priests with a mission to administer Christ and its salvation saw women's roles as threatening to their implementation of the religion. Upon return to the Vatican, authorities demanded the Pontiff "put an end to such foolery!" A matriarchal society went against their patriarchal system, and prevented the conversion of savages. It was a time when the term "witch doctor" helped those practicing traditional beliefs and customs to be pointed out and punished by death. Muskwa recalled her first sick reaction to hearing about the "Burning Times" in Europe where women like the Aboriginal "witch doctors" were burned alive for practicing healing rites. Today, Muskwa acknowledged the elderly woman inside of her. She honored the past, the present and looked forward to the future. As nightfall quietly descended upon her, she slipped inside of her tent. It was time to crawl under the covers and dream about faraway places.

The teaching in this chapter is about the power of words and about a woman's connection to her inner-child. When growing up, a woman's imagination might have characters such as fairies, unicorns, pixies, wild horses, sprites, little people, faraway places, people and the ancient elders. In the world of magic, the discovery of make-believe people and places consumed her, and while she played, she acted them out. Eventually the adults around her began to program her, "there is no such thing as magic!" The voices from faraway places in the world of make-believe and imagination lessen until they eventually fade into the background of her subconscious taking on a hidden camouflage called "creativity" where the "grandmother within" resides. An elder from an eastern Ojibway community who carried the traditional women's teachings told Muskwa;

> *"Children who speak from this center are known to be wise beyond their years, and speak from this place well into their adulthood until reaching their eldership. In some women, the place within them is open and receptive to the grandmother within, and for others it remains desolate awaiting discovery."*

The conflict began with the subconscious programming inflicted upon us as children by adults and its end resulted in stress and confusion about our life. When Muskwa was growing up she was too young to understand how a "witch doctor takes away sickness," but not too young to decide a "witch doctor couldn't be trusted" because someone told her it was witchcraft and evil. The messages confused her and created extreme stress until clarification of the origin of the word was unveiled to her. Its origin stems from the "1869 to 1951 Canadian Indian Act" which made it illegal to practice Aboriginal customs and culture which included any and all spiritual practices. For eighty-two years traditional healing conducted by Aboriginal medicine people was considered to be a pact with "Satan" or the "Prince of Darkness" and considered satanic. Despite the word's meaning and origin the term, "Witch Doctor" was incorporated into her culture, and meant "healer" in English.

Chapter Summary

The importance of understanding the power of words and the connotations they carry is crucial in acknowledging not just your vision of the story but that of others…their story. The caregivers in Muskwa's past knew what they were doing but lacked the awareness around their behavior. By becoming mindful of behaviors, Muskwa was able to separate confusing mental and emotional behaviors of her father, mother, and brother from their person. Taking it to another level, Muskwa realized there were times her family loved her and the relationships weren't "always abusive." In order to release yourself from the burden you carry, the first step is in "knowing their story" and then follow up with "forgiveness." Forgiveness is work, but it's for someone who wants to get off the "treadmill" and move on with life.

Exercise

1 **In your journal answer the question, "What is your reaction to the meaning of the grandmother within?"**

2 In the Aboriginal communities the importance of the four quadrants: EAST – Spiritual, SOUTH – Emotional, WEST – Physical and NORTH – Mental helps us relate to an intricate balance within our lives. If, for example, there is more emphasis on all quadrants except the spiritual, an imbalance is created affecting all four areas.

   a Focusing on the grandmother within you, what does she look like? Sound like?

   b Beginning with the first quadrant EAST, ask the grandmother within to guide you in your writing a complete answer to the questions above in "a"

3 **Guidelines to free writing:**

   a Complete one quadrant of the four each day

   b Ask your "grandmother within" to guide you in your writing

   c Use intuition, and lock out the CRITIC and SELF-JUDGEMENT, or the CRITICAL SELF during your writing.

   d Have fun!

SIX

FINDING MY CIRCLE (PTSD)

Woman

M uskwa moved about the kitchen while washing the morning dishes. She was listening to the radio. Once again the voice of a newsman reported more unmarked grave sites of Aboriginal children had been found behind a nearby residential school. On the air frequent topics included residential school effects, and the horrific abuses inflicted upon its children.

Discussions had been held at varying levels by the scientists, researchers, psychologists, and other professionals. It was alarming to Muskwa because she had never been exposed to the truths of the residential school she had attended briefly as a child. Due to the outcry coming from communities across Canada, the government could no longer ignore the generational effects of sexual, psychological, emotional, mental and spiritual abuses inflicted on First Nation people in an attempt to "kill the Indian in the child," a strategy orchestrated by Duncan Campbell Scott deputy minister of Indian Affairs. An apology from the Canada's Prime Minister of Canada, the Right Honorable Stephen Harper, came to Aboriginal people on June 11, 2008. Financial retribution to the residential school survivors began in 2007 and a shift in educating society began a process of reconciliation for Aboriginal survivors to begin a healing process. "Or did it?" wondered Muskwa. She read a doctoral thesis that made references to generational "post-traumatic stress syndrome" or PTSD by Professor Stan Graff who said, *"Trauma becomes so unbearable, it emotionally pushes us to 'check out' or to separate ourselves from the pain."* In other words, to avoid the pain we find ways to forget. Unfortunately, the pain that still exists, and gets buried where it sits on "pause" in the psyche of the individual. That part of us becomes trapped until we can look at the pain in a safe environment. When someone experiences trauma at the age of six, their emotional development and maturity remains stuck at six years old. Children in pain grow into adulthood and the trauma gets stored away. The energy concealed in pain is hidden under shame. After much thought on the various writings, Muskwa referred to her pain as a "generational holding pattern" handed down to her from her mother's and grandmother's DNA.

Muskwa recalled the first time she experienced her own holding pattern during a sweat lodge ceremony. In the intensity of the heat came a feeling of complete hopelessness surfacing from within her. Her physical senses felt restrained like a paralysis coming from extreme terror. Frozen, riveted to one spot, she recalled how difficult it was to move; it was as if every muscle in her body was immobilized. She tried to understand the origin of the feelings after the sweat lodge but couldn't recall incidences in her life that would bring on such terror. In consultation with her elderly teachers she was told, "At a child's age of one to three years old he/she would be limited in vocabulary and have very few words". As an adult she was re-experiencing a trauma but would be unable to describe the abuse because of the by the lack of words. Her traditional teacher shared two ways children could inherit post-generational trauma. The first occurred in vetro while the baby was in the womb. Mother and baby share sustenance from the physical development through nutrition, to the sympathetic nervous system a safe environment, and to the brain and nervous system development derived from nurturing – a spiritual aspect of human growth. *We are what we eat, drink, think speak or believe.* She thought to herself. Aboriginal peoples created protocols (way of doing things), feasts, and ceremonies to honor mother and child. The system supported by the communities gave birth to the well-being of newly born baby and its mother. The older ones in the community, or elders, knew that if mom experienced a horrific event or traumatic experience prior to pregnancy, the memories became stored as energy. When the occurrence remains unresolved, the emotional and mental energies encapsulate the memory to prevent any recall or awareness of its source. Muskwa remembered how the elders pointed out the absorption of this energy became cellular building blocks retained in muscles and bones in the creation of new life. A reawakening of the trauma is caused by being "triggered by a similar event" and sometimes a ricochet of memories could be released. Muskwa thought about trauma and her body's ability to "put the message on hold till later."

The second way for trauma to be transmitted to a child was through the mother's energy field. Muskwa recalled how her youngest daughter clung to her from the time she was born until she was seven years old. She had a child who needed to have her mother in sight at all times. Her daughter "Morning Star" would grow out of the need for this connection by the age of seven. When Morning Star was sitting on Muskwa's lap and someone approached her, her daughter pushed with her hands, any person who neared them. At times Muskwa found the connection discomforting; when she was feeling at unease with someone, Morning Star picked up on it.

Muskwa's elders referred regularly to the energy around us as an aura. In children, the aura isn't fully developed until the age of seven. A child develops a sense of boundaries and self-identity through the mother's energy and until she/he is ready to disconnect from the mother. If a mother experienced trauma in her life and it is stored in her psyche, the child will receive the information through the energy field of the mother. Or, if the mother was abused in front of the child, the child registers it in their consciousness as something that has *"occurred to them."* From this information, Muskwa realized how her awareness had grown and her ability to trace the origins of particular fears when they surfaced.

As the radio announcer blurted out different ad campaigns, his voice faded into the background. Muskwa moved about her house doing small chores. While she watered her plants, she pondered on trauma and its effects on her life. She recalled dreams about being stalked by an unknown predator. From the time she was around seven years old to about thirty-two years old she hated the night. Sleep didn't come easily! There was a time in her life when she wondered "What was wrong with her? Why did her mind register fear at night?" She dug for the answer, but she couldn't find it. At night lying awake she saw shadows moving in the dark, and a feeling of terror would envelope her. After attending sweat lodge sessions and seeking out the wisdom of various elders, Muskwa began to identify fears that didn't belong to her. She now acknowledged her childhood upbringing came from adults who were residential school survivors.

Traditional teachings that once held practical guidance and altruistic wisdom of the land became garbled and mixed up by generational trauma. The spirits who visited the gifted healers were now considered satanic and its messages could only come from the devil. Animals who once carried messages of direction, transition or change, now were omens of impending death. Women's menstrual cycles became toxic and poisonous to the men and how could anyone protect themselves from the invisible things that walked at night? Aboriginal urban legends took place of wisdom. If a person saw a wolf running towards a neighbor's tree, it was indication the person(s) living there were going to receive bad news. Or maybe a bird hit auntie's window and she would wait for the worse news to come. Over and over, her mother Red Tree cited messages of doom and despair, and the doom became recycled in belief. A paradigm preventing life's joy!

As all women move into healing of their past, the attack on women's body image and connection to her sexuality will uncover abuses hidden under the guise of incomplete teachings around moon cycles and menopause. Today, traditional knowledge is being freely shared verbally, and the distortions from post-trauma victims are healing from sexual or spiritual abuses, as they bring their stories into the light.

As a child, Muskwa recalled the largest part of her healing was associated with abandonment that came about when her mother partied and left her young brother and herself alone. The overwhelming fear and scary stories told by adults were enough to open any child's flood gates to other energies present at the time. Muskwa saw as a child facing fear of being alone, the third eye prematurely opened too early. In its efforts to protect her, her body responded to the terror by flooding her physical with brain chemicals like morphine to sedate, then the trigger alerted her body to anesthetize her body prior to death wrote by author Linda Kohanov in *The Tao of Equus: A Woman's Journey of Healing and Transformation through the Way of the Horse.*" The feelings of abandonment she felt as a child would resurface in her youth life in the form of "suicidal tendencies," it's origin from her inner child's understanding, "I'm not wanted." Once completely understood at this level a new paradigm, "I shouldn't be here" began to take effect on her as a young woman that took shape in "cervical dysplasia III." Each of these levels of healing, Muskwa recalled how it felt to reclaim herself as whole once again!

Muskwa began to make her bed, and proceeded to fold her laundry. Really what she had done throughout the years was to find her center. When she gave it more thought, it meant she needed to look at her beliefs. Almost like sorting through the laundry, it was like "pairing socks." There was an oddball sock, no mate that seemed to find its way back into her basket. With a quick move, she threw it in the garbage, and that's exactly what she did with a number of fears she had that weren't her own. One good example was "not to think about hurting someone when you're angry." She was told her anger would "kill them." At the head of the lesson was, "you are never allowed to express anger safely." When she did, she would receive a slap from her mother. There was no way to express the anger because tears were considered a weakness. After a length of time it was easier to internalize it and become a master at aloneness by separating self from others. Another was, "don't cry because it makes you weak." Or "A tough Indian never cries." The set of lessons took her spiraling as a failure in the school grounds. She was told to ignore the bullies but it never worked. Instead of the "toughening up", her lack of response to the bullying invited more bullying.

The quiet embodiment of PTSD passed down to her became awakened through the verbal humiliation she received. Name calling included "wagon burner," "squaw" and "half breed" as well as "good for nothing." The name calling hurt her; she didn't understand what any of the words meant.

For Muskwa, it kept a lifelong dialogue alive in her head, "What's wrong with me?" She had wondered many times if blonde hair and blue eyes would make a difference? The energy of the words directed at her so long ago, now unnecessary to hold onto. She realized she once was a child who was susceptible to "others bad behavior" and could free it from her self-identity. The faces long gone buried in the past, she would no longer allow its effect on her.

As time went on, she began to loathe her weakness and dug for a memory of the terror she felt because the feelings that cascaded within her in the present didn't make sense. She was raised off-reserve, her father bought a house; he was hard working and her mother stayed home to raise Muskwa and Twin Eagle. The indescribable terror she knew was not a normal fear, one that got triggered by an offensive word or person. Her reaction created feelings others described as "exaggerated." It would become evident to her that the repression she was taught created an overload, and when it needed words there was too much to express. Muskwa likened her feelings to that of the falling away of a hillside during a heavy rain, where the earth pours forward with no direction. While she moved about the house pondering, she realized any person triggered by an activity, incident or person, was not going to think logically about what just happened! The only other thing that might be different about traumatic fear is it might send a person into a corner to hide.

As a child, like most children on the school ground, she was bullied. The bullies called her stupid, and the "D's" she brought home on her report card meant groundings. Along the way she developed defense mechanisms to cope. One defense was to write everything down. It was easier for her to remember than committing them to memory. She recalled feeling like a hostage to pen and paper. There were times she forgot to take notes on something, and recalled how inefficient she felt when she couldn't answer a question around the notes she took. The effort it took to maintain the writing and the organization of her thoughts resulted in emotional breakdowns. She found herself crying relentlessly but didn't understand why. After some digging, she identified a pattern in relationship to her thinking. "You're too stupid to learn," something she heard adults repeat to her. It was also an era in her life where psychology was in its infancy, and verbal abuse was still considered normal or a norm within society. When she was triggered by present verbal putdowns, it surfaced layers of past abusive words. The pain went deep, too deep, and she couldn't understand the depth of its reoccurrence until an elder suggested it may come from a source called "DNA memories," a place where ancient wisdom, songs and legends are stored. She had an image of her inner-child psyche as a sponge, soaking up energy from conversations, body language and inter-actions from those around her. For her, there was a huge void or abyss in traditional training around memories by the elders. She recalled connecting the stories about the rhythm of the drum her ancestors played to what scientists refer to as DNA and how the information created a transitional shift in her awareness about the origin of fear.

When Muskwa entered her own circle, every step she took in her healing brought her one step closer to what elders called, "coming into your own." No longer was she afraid of the night, the dark secrets held by the mothers before her. All had been taken care of through hard emotional work and prayer. The need to be someone else also began to disappear, she noted to herself. Muskwa felt a unique sense of herself and her space. The craziness that came from the sleepless nights, and the thirst for alcohol or drugs she used to numb the fear became non-existent. On her personal journey of healing, wellness and balance occurred in all four quadrants of her spiritual, emotional, physical and mental well-being.

The healing journey is not for the light-hearted. Muskwa reflected on the number of friends she lost to alcohol and drugs caused by unspoken secrets. For some, healing is a phase of life that calls in the "tracker." The Tshilqot'in people had the ability to identify children who would become expert trackers in the bush. Today, the gift of tracking has transitioned and changed to accommodate the times; it can be applied to the sixth sense. This is the surreal ability to track animal life to its present use in tracking answers for our healing. An expert tracker could tell you in what direction the herd came from and where the herd was headed, except the allegory for the herd is now the origin of pain. For Muskwa, her ancestral sense to hunt found her digging deep within herself to uncover the pain and bring it to the light. In her quest to heal, Muskwa transformed her victimized and abusive character by taking responsibility for her decisions in life. By looking at her learning models – coping mechanisms, beliefs and habits – she was able to establish a healing plan to "look after herself."

Muskwa looked up at the clock in the bedroom after making her bed, and decided all this thinking and reminiscing of her past made her hungry. Moving towards the kitchen she thought about the dried meat, and dried salmon her grandmother gave to her when she was a child. As her mouth watered she thought to herself, "And the best was her bannock! Now I'm really hungry!" she said aloud to herself.

Chapter Summary

By looking at what you believe, how it affects others, and how you show up in the world, do recognize the courage it takes to heal. It's the reason why this book is called "Walking in Your Own Power" because responsibility, and the commitment to heal, are sought out by few. The longer your programming has been within you, the longer it will be to redefine yourself. Start each day with something new that you would like to change and commit to. Start out trying a few of the questions below that Muskwa incorporated into her own journal entries to begin her quest to heal.

Exercise 1

Identify a belief that is holding you back

Examples: *"I have to have money to make money."* OR *"I'm not good at a lot of things."*

What or who is the origin of this belief?

Does it serve you? Does the belief cause you problems? How?

Is there a hidden meaning behind the belief? Is the belief kind?

Does the belief give life to others? Is it helpful? (The interpretation of "Give Life" means the act of doing something for others or yourself that makes you feel good.)

Do you find the belief motivates you to investigate in its origin? Why? Or Why not?

Exercise 2

Once you find the answers to the question above, how can you rewrite your paradigm into a positive statement?

Example: *"Money is abundant in my life and flows freely to me."* OR *"I am making changes in my life."*

When will you begin to apply positive affirmations to your daily life?

Identify and write in your journal what you will do to apply a new and positive belief.

Write down the date you will start and end the practice to embed this empowering belief into your daily life.

Choose one belief, or word and become mindful of its impact to you and others. Write this in your journal.

SEVEN

ORDERING IN

The Child Within

I t was late summer, the sky was filled with grey, poplar leaves flitted back and forth in the gentle wind as the crispness of early morning filled the atmosphere of earth's landscape. Quietly as usual, Muskwa moved about her kitchen, dicing, chopping and grating vegetables for her modern day "trapper's soup." As she tossed the bologna chunks into the soup's broth she felt her late mother's presence for a moment. In Muskwa's late teens it was a soup her late mother made when the budget was tight. At that time, wild meat was a luxury most Aboriginal people living in the city didn't own. Some of her family made light of the affordable staple by calling it, "flame min yon." While not the top-of-the-line sirloin steak, it was tasty and an equally decadent food that helped families get from one paycheck to another. At big gatherings, people from all over the nations sat laughing whole heartedly referring to the Indian staple as "tube steak" or "kubassa." The use of words jokingly used to exploit the possible meanings of "bologna" as a food of the rich, and the laughter took their focus off their struggles or hardships. It was a time to laugh it all off because laughter was healing.

Muskwa lifted the lid on her "trapper's soup;" her ancestors would have used fireweed leaves, lily root tabor, chickweed and other wild plants. "If they had vegetables from the garden, they would have used vegetables!" she thought to herself with a smile. Then she heard her auntie's voice from the past, "*An occasional ground squirrel or two made it even better!*" Muskwa grimaced at the thought, recalling her late mother always saying to her, "*I spoiled you, I raised you like a city woman.*"

The art of hunting seemed to disappear amidst the younger generation who now had a different mode of transportation outside of the horse! Young people now owned all-terrain vehicles or ATV's she called "northern metal horses." Metal on rubber wheels that could go anywhere, up hillsides into the mountains, through marshes, bogs and waters, the vehicle had very few limits…except for the use of gas. A jerry can could be attached to the new pony and off into the wilderness they could go. *What about ecology? Or leaving carbon footprint?* She recalled a document sent to her on the effects of mining and the drilling for oil. What about the "total set of GHG or greenhouse gas emission effects and damage to the ecosystem's medicines caused directly and indirectly by an individual or company driving ATV's on precious territory preserved for future generations?

Muskwa sighed. There was a way of life that once needed the energy of horses and the wilderness guide's knowledge to teach others about the delicate balance of the land. The importance about bush knowledge, and how to move around on the mountain were time worn experiences that needed protection. How could knowledge passed down from one grandfather to the next generation be replaced by an "iron pony?" People of the Caribou recognized wilderness guides as, "outfitters." The brazen physical and inner strength of Tshilqot'in men and women who were brought up by the land, raised by the land, were guiding its people and visitors around the land. The outfitters vast knowledge of the wildlife migratory paths and their active protection from overhunting gives one the feeling of mother earth's patrol officer on duty. Without them, the wilderness goes unpoliced and become susceptible to big game hunters who fly in to harvest prize antlers or the biggest "big horn" sheep, moose or deer of their picking without conscience! Like a wild rose that grows on the hillside in gravel, an Tshilqot'in outfitter was noted as a noble rider and one with his/her animal the horse. *What could be more romantic than his/her silhouette amidst the mountain tapestry?* She thought to herself. A Tshilqot'in outfitter who fits the personae of Buffalo Bill from the Plains who adapts and bears shifts between mountain altitudes and changing mountain weather patterns and a provider of food to the community through a hunt. Muskwa began to laugh to herself, "A scene far away from the Extra Foods Grocery Store hunter she had become!"

The memory of her family hunting in the mountains filled her senses with nostalgia. A burning ember of pride pulsated within her chest. Muskwa's thoughts were brought back to the present as she placed cedar on the stove to boil. Soon she could smell the cedar as it filled her living space. The word "adaptation" and the tools of assimilation had almost completely wiped out cultural practices and earth pharmaceutical knowledge her people once held. Again her thoughts were taken back to "ordering in." In today's society, most of her people had become accustomed to "quick fixes." Got a headache? Get a pill from the drug store. Prevent the flu, get a flu shot. Make food tastier, a little dash of this, and a whole lot of sugar. From plastic bags, to ready-made doughnuts. From healing to instant recovery in a three-day workshop. Drive here, drive there and the image of riding the horse, or foraging for berries or leaves with a group of women began to fade into the background of societal progress.

The cedar on the stove was ready to be turned off, and she would soak in it later to relieve her muscle ache. Muskwa sat down, her memories were strong this morning. She reached over to grab the small cotton bag with her smudge bowl items, and took out all the contents. Within the smudge bowl she placed sage for clearing, juniper for protection, sweet grass to sooth and tobacco as an offering to the spirits. As she prayed, she thanked Creator for the messages and the answers filtering into her being from the spirit world.

Her thoughts went back to a time when she had attended a conference and first heard the term "inner-child." At first she could not integrate its information or understand how to apply it to her own life. Later she discovered the "inner-child" was metaphorical. It represented her growing up years; the part of her that had not been heard, seen, or treated in a healthy nurturing way when she was a child. She began to understand how the feelings of being ignored, abandoned, or that of unresolved feelings got buried and carried into her adult life. The patterns showed up when there were lack of healthy boundaries with herself and others in her life. When inner-child work became the buzz in alternative medicine, self-help books, audio and workshops sprung up all over the place. As she reflected on her healing of her wounded child, she raised her eyebrows in admiration of herself – *"it took more time than a self-help workbook!"*

Through work with her traditional community, the payback for her was the hidden jewel she discovered in herself at a much deeper level. Here inner-child replaced her mother's friends 'the three monkeys' with three different gifts; *"see no evil"* transformed into visual artistry, *"hear no evil"* became transformed as a published author and *"speak no evil"* converted to an empowerment speaker. At first she thought the dark images of the past were the only things she would ever see! *"Was I ever going to stop crying?"* she recalled as she thought about layers of undisclosed feelings that came from mixed messages that needed to be deciphered; those memories of neglect, abandonment, abuse from her mother's rage, and later on in her childhood from her mother's alcoholism, and how it taught her it was not safe *"to cry."* Her mother's Red Tree had been disciplined with "force" characteristic of residential school education. In school grade one, Muskwa recalled some of her peers getting their knuckles rapped with a ruler; it was a time when "corporal punishment," was supported by society. Other forms of student punishment included spankings with a ruler in the principal's office. Canadian families were conditioned to parent in an authoritarian or "drill sergeant" manner, and spankings were normal forms of discipline. Behavioral correction that resulted in bruises, scuffs, broken bones or death were normal and went unreported. Muskwa's thoughts led her to thinking about effects abusive punishment had on her setting personal and professional boundaries as an adult. A lifetime of learning, a lifelong journey it had been.

Muskwa moved into her living room, took the book she was reading off the coffee table and quickly made herself comfortable. She reread a passage penned by a gifted Sioux writer named Ron Zeilinger who portrayed Morning Star so beautifully;

> *"Just before the sun rises, there is a star standing alone, shining brightly in the east. A star that is there when the sun comes up. Venus the planet of love and its twin Dawn star are one and alike in each other. Morning Star, there at the place where the sun comes up that our generations will have light as they walk the sacred path. You lead the dawn as it walks forth, and also the day which follows with its light which is knowledge."*

—LAKOTA LIFE, 2013.

She broke from her reading as she reminisced about the elder she met at a gathering some time ago. According to "Two Turtle Woman," the Morning Star brought light followed by the dew upon the grasses of the earth, and was the cause of the birth of all living things on earth. She likened it to the conception of a child, nurtured in embryonic fluid. It was a star, pure at its state just like the "child within." Two Turtle Woman's friend who had been present that day was an avid beader who added further knowledge, "the symbol of Venus is also a five-pointed star and we bead it as a five-petal rose!" Muskwa shifted herself, and moved around to get more comfortable. Soon it would be time to soak in her cedar concoction to ease the ache in her body.

The doorbell rang, Muskwa placed the book back onto the coffee table. As she opened the door she could see her smiling friend's face. "Come on in Shalone! Coffee is on" she said excitedly. The two disappeared into the kitchen while Shalone shared the festivities and events she had with her grandchildren. "Did you know the youngest who is four is learning how to speak Spanish? I'm not kidding, something to do with the Ipad! Can you believe it? I'm so shocked and amazed at the same time. When I was that age, I was kicked outside when my mother's nerves wore down!" she laughed loudly. Muskwa laughed, "I had an overprotective father who was too afraid to let me do anything. It was a good day when we could go to the park! I don't know what was with him, but maybe it had something to do with him being raised in the thirties? Who knows?"

Shalone took a sip of her coffee and said, "We had to keep our-selves busy outside. I remember playing with sticks. Draw a line in the dirt for roads, and the sticks took on a walking talking dude!" she said with a smile.

"Did your parents come from a big family?" Muskwa asked.

"Yes, both mother and father had many siblings. Mother had ten brothers and sisters, while my father had around six." Shalone said.

"My dad was raised a prairie child, who had two other brothers and three sisters. He told me he had to walk to a small school house some distance, didn't matter rain, snow or freezing temperatures. The school house held around ten to fifteen children who also walked from neighboring farms. One time he shared how children like himself carried lunch in sacks or metal pails to school." Muskwa replied.

"Did you get an allowance?" Muskwa asked.

"Yes, we got around two to four dollars every other week for completing our chores." She said.

"I don't feel bad then, as my dad gave me five dollars twice a month when I was ten years old. I really had to save up for the things I wanted and it taught me a lot about how to budget!" shared Muskwa.

"I'm going to get another cup of coffee, want some more?" her friend asked.

"No, I'm fine for the moment." replied Muskwa. After her friend Shalone sat down and got comfortable again, the conversation returned.

"OMG! I was so funny as a kid! I used to read Archie comic books, did you ever read those? She asked her friend.

"Yes! They were the highlight and I could hardly wait to read the next one!" she said.

"I went on a mission to collect coupons that became my wish list. One I filled out was to purchase sea monkeys." Muskwa laughed.

"I remember seeing the pictures, they looked interesting. I never had a chance to buy them. Did you fill the coupon out and mail it?" Shalone asked.

"Yes, I filled the coupon out but there was a problem with stamps. We had envelopes in the house but no stamps. One of my other hobbies was stamp collecting. I used to buy bags of filled with stamps from all over the world. Some of the stamps looked brand new, fresh from the post office, so I reused them!" she said in a roar of laughter.

"You're kidding?" Shalone asked.

"No, I got away with it until the envelope was returned one day with memo from the post office stating re-used stamps was punishable by law or something like that! I have to say, shopping from a comic allowed me to have different experiences than most children! I even ordered a hermit crab one time. I was disappointed, it was delivered to my door step in a box, in cold weather. Needless to say it was freeze dried!" Muskwa roared in laughter.

"Way too funny!" Shalone shrieked with laughter.

After the two calmed down Muskwa said, "I found a way to become a part of the world outside of those walls. Yeah, while my father was fearful, I learned through my determination a new skill, one we call sales and marketing today. I learned how to pitch the idea to my dad, and if it didn't go through, I came back the next day with a fresh strategy. I worked on convincing him that whatever I was going to do would not only benefit him, but benefit me. Most times the answer remained the same but other times it got her a few extra dollars for recreational activities at school." Muskwa said as she reminisced.

"I admire how you were able to grasp what you learned from your father! If I were to look at my interest in fashion it would come from those days my mother dressed me up like a Barbie Doll! I don't know if you remember the scratchy type material petticoats were made from? When she put me in that I couldn't help but scratch because the material dug right into my skin! If that wasn't all in the dolling up of Shalone here, she had to make ringlets in my hair! Oh I hated it when she tore up and old sheet in strips to then twist my hair into the cloth strips! Then there were saddle shoes. Mind you, I did love the shoes. I didn't' like it when I got scuffs on them, and she would be going on about how much they cost. The shoes had an elastic for buckles and kept breaking! You would think the way she fussed over me I'd avoid the latest fashion trend as an adult! It's where I developed my fashion sense! I now offer fashion critique to a local magazine's dresses, and shoes." She laughed again.

The two quickly wound down and Shalone had a list of things to do in her day. They each hugged each other, and her friend left. Muskwa gathered the empty cups smiling to herself, her grin from ear to ear. She realized the balance to her life came from her childhood experimentations, the people she met along the way, the books and the events she attended throughout her life. The collection of knowledge a compilation of good and bad experiences she needed in order to develop "discernment." The wisdom to see the true nature of things, the ability to distinguish between what was real and what wasn't. She noted as she got older her intuition drew her to the right places, and over a period of time provided her with insight, or a way of seeing her world with different eyes. Characteristics like creativity, imagination, holistic thinking, intuition, arts, rhythm, non-verbal communication, visualizations and daydreaming all hall marks from her childhood. She realized her educators at the time taught from a linear perspective, a grueling environment for a right brain learner whose ability was in creativity! Like her friend who hated being dressed up like a Barbie Doll she realized she had put her abilities this morning into perspective, *she learned how to teach others how to teach themselves using their creativity.*"

Chapter Summary

While Muskwa touched on corporal punishment, she provided a brief explanation between the differences of using "force" and that of "discipline." We as readers got a sense while one left bruises the other may or may not have included a spanking, "discipline" described loving correction. Through her chapter we got a sense that we could learn how to fish, instead of becoming dependent on someone to fish for us. From the chapter on "Ordering In" we could conclude healing wasn't meant to be a fast food take out. Instead, a life's journey to explore patterns around *we are what we think, feel or do* its effect on our daily interactions with the world. A lot of times when we are in a fix as an adult, the clue may come from the inner child who is still providing parental information from her/his age of four or five years old. She emphasized that healing took a longer time, and the need for patience in uncovering patterns and to seek nurturing environments.

Exercise

By initiating activities to invite the inner-child to create, we can begin to reprogram, and value our intuition through music, drama and artistic expression. Movement has a way of helping us move out of our comfort zones to share our "spark" with others.

1   Buy a small sketchbook. Sit down for 10 to 15 minutes every day to draw your feelings. Express them in shapes, or experiment by painting or coloring them in with various colors. Doodle, shade, paint or whatever it takes to bring the child within you out to create. (Too often the answers we seek come from this child.) Like Muskwa, think about the ways you bring out the creativity in others.

2   Hold a "Card Buffet" night. Invite all your friends. Ask them to bring embellishments, and or card accessories to share with the group. You can provide the basics to make a simple handmade card together.

3   Collaborative Dance & Paint night – Invite your friends, or co-workers to an evening of color. Set out trays of different colors, glitter, acrylic gels, and or pastes. You can add rollers, trays, brushes etc. Cover one wall fully with white table paper, and secure with tape or tacks. When your company comes instruct them to become "mimes" no words are exchanged in this activity. Get your guests started, ask them to dip their hands into various colored paint, and to place on the wall paper in random fashion when the music begins. They will continue their exercise through two songs before the brushes, gels and other tools are used in the collaborative painting.

Note: Fast paced music is better for the movement. Whether it's Rock N' Roll, African, Aboriginal or of another culture works. When it's fast paced we have less of a tendency to think. Dance and Paint! Have Fun exploring with the inner-child!

EIGHT

BROKEN ARROW

South Direction: Emotional

On a cold wintery January day, she stood there watching the fire consume the last of her late mother's items. It was customary in her culture to burn all belongings a person wore or touched prior to their death. Things like boots, a coat, clothing, or their favorite items such as a necklace, rings, wallet, key ring or medications had to be burned. Burning of the items was insurance the loved one would have no reason to look back and no distraction of the spirit as it journeyed back to the spirit world. As the flames shot upwards, there was peace in knowing her late mother's spirit would not get stuck on earth looking for any of her objects. A small number of the family came together in the evening quietly, they were spent from the days of travel, preparation and organization of the wake. Not too far from the fire across the road in house, a group of people had pooled together to party. Through the darkness, Muskwa saw vehicle headlights, the roar of engines, and the squeal of tires on the ice as the drivers raced up and down the icy road. There were others who drank outside who hollered and screamed profanities that filled the air. For some reason this had become a norm for grieving in the community. She paid no attention as she watched the flames dance and the light move back and forth into the night.

All of a sudden a vehicle drove up the gravel drive way, windows rolled down with the loud music of "Nazareth" belting from the cab. As the driver stepped on the gas the broken muffler roared loudly, and it caught everyone's attention just before the slamming of the vehicle brakes. Out fell two drunken young adults, so intoxicated it was a wonder the driver of the vehicle was still functioning! At the fire the men that stood by Muskwa, along with other women at the campfire, remained quiet and unresponsive to the visitors. Muskwa's anger arose when she saw how close they had come to hitting her vehicle! She watched one of the young men stagger to a fence within sight to begin to urinate! Her eyes shifted to the other swaying gently back and forth in the dark by a tree. Muskwa approached the intoxicated man who was the driver and said in a stern and quiet voice, "You had best move your truck and leave."

The drunken young man slowly raised his head, latched eyes with her, "You f'n bitch! Who do you think you are! I don't have to listen to you, you bitch! Why don't you just shut the f* up! I have a good mind to punch you out. You're not even family!" he screamed at her. Muskwa stood quietly unwavering from the verbal attack. She had become accustomed to dealing with drunks but quickly felt anger rushing through her veins. In all respect, behavior like this at a wake? She felt her rage spike, and with a slow methodical breath she inhaled to calm herself. Muskwa knew the outcome would be based on her reaction. Meanwhile, the other young man after relieving himself by a corral fence staggered past the both of them. He repeated apologies about his drinking and that of his cousin. "Sorry man, we're just all f'd up!" he said. Muskwa's recalled her first thought, "And we're expected to put up with the drunken behavior and be nice! When did we as a people make it alright for someone else to abuse us? Why is this acceptable?" No one by the fire moved, she saw disengaged relatives, it was if the scene was only being played out on her behalf. Finally, as the young man screamed, "F you!" a few more times a relative interceded the cussing and began to talk to him. An air of kindness, and understanding came from the voice in the dark as he or she spoke with the drunken young adult. Eventually, after about an hour of conversation the young men got into the vehicle and drove past Muskwa's vehicle.

Muskwa lifted her head from her journal writing. She was sitting at her kitchen table reading excerpts of her journal that were penned six months ago. She was made out to be the bad guy, and the drunken young man the hero. Really? If we were to call this for what it was, wasn't it enabling? The young man was soothed and comforted for his wrong doing, making it alright for him to abuse women and community members. What message did that send to everyone else? After the writing she read, *"We will accept the things we don't want in our lives by keeping them alive. We will fight to protect it even if it means sacrificing our lives."* Then she wondered, *"Why do we do that? Why did I do that in the past?"* When her mother was drunk and disorderly, it was easier to ignore the behavior or leave the house. As she moved about the house, she pondered heavily on addiction. Muskwa began to clean her bedroom, when she turned, her image from the mirror reflected back to her. She was in deep thought about setting personal boundaries. There was a rule a friend shared with her one time, she now referred to it as: Rule #1 *"To each his own, unless it affects me personally."* She recalled the difficulties she had in setting personal boundaries, calling upon not only her courage to be assertive when decision making or safety was violated. Rule #2 *"It isn't just our right, but our duty to take responsibility for how others treat us."* The application of the rule changed the way she wanted to be treated by others. Rule #3 No more crazy-making! *"We do not have the power to **make** anyone do anything.* Too often she heard "You make me angry!" or "You make me drink!" She grew up believing she had some kind of evil power to make people do things—and it gave way to other's falsely accusing her for things she never did. A pattern of "crazy-making!"

Muskwa's interest in the Mohawk began when she heard a story about how the Iroquois Confederacy's five groups decided to come together around the years 1400 to 1600. A prophet came to the people and emphasised the need for all five groups – The Mohawk, the Oneida, the Onondaga, the Cayuga, and the Seneca – to come together as one to become impenetrably strong. The prophet could not get everybody's attention until he used his arrows in demonstration. He showed how fragile one arrow, the symbol of one group, snapped easily when he bent it over his knee. Then taking five arrows he repeated the same and the arrows did not break. The Mohawk did well, in fact she heard the United States Senate gave acknowledgment in the 1980's to the Iroquois Confederacy's contribution in the development of the constitution. The image of a "broken arrow" and its bundle of arrows remained in her memory for a very long time. In her own community the efforts of traditional teachings and the revitalization of cultural ways had slowly taken hold over the years, and the numbers of homicides, suicides and addictions had dropped. However, in the 1970's to 1980's youth suicide rates and high school dropout rates were at an all-time high in Aboriginal communities.

Muskwa approached the coffee pot, she poured herself another cup. Abuse? "You can bandage an open wound to protect it from infection and leave it for a day. If you forget to change it daily, the wound becomes infected. Any number of things can happen with an infection depending on the length of time it goes untreated." The drunken, screaming young person had become a good example of woundedness. He had also become a visual image of the broken arrow in the bundle.

Muskwa sat down, returned to her journal writing and thought to herself, "That young man represented something that was missing" If she could just put her finger on it. While a majority of her family spoke their own language, but many more that lived off-reserve who didn't speak the language. The second insight was the loss of traditional values and customs within the communities on-reserve and off-reserve. All of a sudden the image of the "broken arrow" nestled in amidst the bundle of arrows started to make sense. At the heart of every culture is its language, one of the main structural pillars for communicating values, beliefs and customs and its importance to the connection to all my relations." Muskwa lifted her head for a moment and penned these words into her journal, *"I am Tshilqot'in or Tshil – (Rock) – qu – (River) – t'in (people of). I am also, Nenqayni or Nen (Earth, land) – qay – (surface) – ni (deni or person)."* As she read what she wrote aloud, she felt the pulse of the words, they soothed her as they rolled off her tongue. Muskwa thought about how the four directions fit within the warrior bow and arrow bundle. In her reflection she saw how the four directions, a living eco-teaching model was a part of each one of us. From her experience, she recognized language needed "storytelling" by the elders. She drifted to a past memory, in front of her sat one of her late elders on a chair. He was introducing a story, "Chungh...Chungh." It meant, "once again." He said he started his stories off in this manner because Chungh, Chungh meant he was the carrier of others' stories. He continued, *"Two men who went hunting in the mountains brought down this big animal they said. In order to keep warm, after they cleaned it they both crawled inside of it to keep warm."* At the time Muskwa had asked the elder if it could have been a Mastodon. There it was, the first story of hunting—one could imagine spear, or bow and arrow? The elder said he had seen a picture of one in a magazine once, and it was a Mastodon. There were no rifles in that period of time when these big animals roamed the earth.

According to her family knowledge, obsidian used for flint and arrowheads were harvested on Anaheim Peak, a volcanic belt in British Columbia. Muskwa was excited with her new revelation. "Can you imagine what a Mastodon hunt might have looked like in the days of the ancestors? Did they use spears? Or did they pack heavier bow and arrows?" she thought to herself. The obsidian arrowhead represented the "language" within the culture. To make one, a bow hunter needed knowledge to create a pointed tip comprised of gradual curve like shapes like that of a mussel shell. She knew an arrowhead maker had to know where to harvest the materials, its preparation, and the techniques to perfect a very sharp missile for hunting. Hunting a mastodon, and failure of the projectile killing the animal could mean the difference between the hunter's life or death. Muskwa saw the obsidian arrowhead in the North of the Medicine Wheel because the material was forged by the Earth's heat (fire) through volcanic activity. In the North, men were given the ability to provide for their families and it is here they formed societies to strengthen the male role. Creator had given them "council" and the gift of "discipline" for themselves and their family. She pondered on fractured teachings that affected Aboriginal parenting in a way that had resulted in giving men direction to apply "force". One good example, "The Rule of Thumb" created in the 1700's gave English men the right to correct their women in a moderate fashion. Nonetheless, it gave way to spousal abuse. According to law, he could use a stick or rod, or bigger than his thumb, as form of mild discipline of his wife or children. Muskwa shuddered, the punishment wasn't too different than corporal punishment within the school system! Today, the law has been obliterated and the punishment an "abusive and a violent" way to teach wrong doing.

Muskwa could see how relationship imbalance between men and women when distinct societal houses that had once been the foundation of tribal justice formed by clans were banned by the government. Instead, both sexes were now grouped together as one in their learning. In the past, women's groups focused on the mastery of "counselling" and "harvesting, and application" of medicines for health issues. While the men held "council" with one another, and traded masteries around hunting, fishing or any other expertise. The arrowhead illustrates women and the element of water. Muskwa revered the water's ability to compress gases in the petrification of the minerals from the earth in the creation of the obsidian. The obsidian, an analogy to the sacredness of her own waters within her body. Through the teachings passed down in the language, a woman learned her connection to the water and its influence by the rhythm of the Moon. In the days of the ancestors, natural light came from the stars, moon and the sun. The effect of fluorescent lighting, and radio waves created from electricity, and modern day appliances knocks women's Moon Cycle off-balance creating sickness. Today's woman has more stress in her life, and less time to look up to "Grandmother Moon" to fill her eyes with the natural spectrum lighting. She needs to watch the moon a few minutes every night when it is full. When she does, her body will spring back to its normal rhythm. The elderly teachers also reminded women in the teaching circles to change the abuse. "*The manipulative abuse continues when men take the roles of the female as his own, in the quest of power. Women! Pick up your bundles and get to work!*" In the circle of "Grandmother Moon" teachings it is a space created for women to heal from sexual, physical, emotional or mental abuse and not be attended by men until they are committed to "healing themselves." In most countries of the world, the Full Moon Ceremony is for women only.

Muskwa got up and moved around. She thought about how the shaft of the arrow was definitely a fitting symbol for "Culture" where beliefs, customs and values create a sense of personal identity. An arrow maker knows his or her wood. Douglas Fir is too heavy because of its granular structure but Ash is an indestructible material. Yet Ash might also make the arrow sail in the air too slowly. Culture is a way of thinking and behavior related to upbringing. She sighed loudly as she recalled a time when finding a street gang was all about fitting in somewhere. The reward for loyalty and bravery was acceptance. Her mind drifted back to the two drunken young men, a sense of unconditional love for them filtered through her being.

The feathers attached to the shaft of the arrow come from water fowl and are iconic of "family", where trust and faith are built. It takes the traditional eye of a teacher to guide us in the right selection of feathers, their attachment to the shaft, and techniques to keep them from falling off. Like parenting, a soft sturdy downy feather will determine which direction the arrow will spin once released from the bow. Too often a beginner will attach a large feather, but its weight will prevent the arrow from releasing from the bow. Some of the grandmothers said the effect of the generational abuses and its anger had created burdens like this in the future generations. Some arrow makers make decisions to change the look of the arrow for ascetic purposes and gravitate to a feather that is too soft, causing the arrow to fall too quickly to the ground after its release. The teachings from the grandmothers indicated colossal change in parenting was caused by a lack of parental guidance caused by fear and then overprotection of their children that created self-entitlement in some of the younger generation.

She moved towards the window, holding her journal in one hand and a pen in the other. One of the elderly men said the integral part of the arrow is the nock or bottom node. The part of the arrow that often gets dismissed because of its size. The nock of the arrow represents "self-identity," because it is the most essential in the community-building process. A bow hunter knows how to properly nock the arrow onto the bowstring. His father's teachings equipped him, he knew if an arrow required excessive force to release the arrow would not be carried by the wind. He has also had the experience of wins and losses in his hunting while out with the men.

To know oneself, his or her capabilities, strengths and weaknesses, developed self-confidence. The bow hunter, male or female, was raised by everyone in a traditional family. To her, the nock was the clan houses. Every family had a particular gift: bear clan – policed the community and/or were medicine healers; sturgeon – became mediators; hoofed clans were warriors; while the small four legged held the position of counsellors. Muskwa had an affinity for the sweat lodge, as it brought to her new meanings to her purpose and her journey. She recalled the day the spirits presented her with a song. It was her clan house welcoming song! It came to her in 1993 while she was gardening. An overwhelming need to bring out her drum filled her. She recalled how the lyrics arrived slowly but the words didn't come until later. Finally, one day her family taught her words to the four directions. Her late mother and Aunt said, *"We say gu?en for up there (North), gunes for down there (South), gu'nish for over there (West), and godah for go that way (East).* How excited she was, combining the words with the rhythm of the hand drum.

At first it felt awkward for her to sing in her language; she did not want anyone to hear. Over a period of time she would overcome her shame and become more comfortable with her Indianness. She smiled not too long ago when she heard someone say, *"When*

GOD happened, you happened. As you took your first breath, GOD took his first breath." The four directions of the medicine wheel had given her structure to find her way back onto the red path of her ancestors. The East characterized birth, as a child our connection to the Creator is maintained through a thread of light that gradually becomes less as a child reaches the age of seven years old.

The South epitomizes air, and feeling like that of pride generated from parental guidance. The correspondence to feeling good generates healthy self-value and fuels "tradition" of our community or people.

She thought about the West, the physical area, and how she felt being raised outside of the language. When she was amidst her mother's family, Muskwa struggled with understanding the meaning of the words and how different tones and glottal changed what was being said. It was a feeling of being very different, one that was described to her as walking between the European and Native worlds.

Looking towards the North of the medicine wheel where the fire beings and the elder's wisdom becomes one with the language. A place where protocols, acceptable behavior and the correct way to live upon the earth with dignity are taught to the community. A time when the snows arrive, temperatures drop, the leaves fall from the trees, and teaches us about death. It is a place where we go into introspection much like the bear does in hibernation. Many communities lack elderly wisdom and guidance, there the analogy of the broken arrow in the bundle might be found.

Chapter Summary

From Muskwa's perspective the two drunken young men represented "enabling abuse in our lives." Additionally, she examined the meaning around, "broken arrow." Reclaiming our personal power through the medicine wheel in our lives, its attributes and problem solving through the use of the traditional justice system. Muskwa touched upon awareness's around healing ourselves and our "belongingness."

Exercise

Step 1

Look at your year of birth, the last number is your clan.
Example: 1995 = 5

0 to 5 = EARTH= visionaries: Bird Clan
1 to 6 = WATER= policemen, healers: bear clan

3 to 8 = NATURE= small four legged
2 to 7 = FIRE= peace makers: hoofed clan

4 to 9 = MINERAL= storytellers, communicators and teachers: fish clan

Step 2

As a group, come together with your clan members. What we're going to do is create the kind of community that sustains energy. You see, everywhere we go people come together for events, celebrations, fundraisers as a "community." Creating community is based on some kind of cosmetology that helps people find their place. It is a quest for identity, of building community and creating a viable relationship with all living things.

Step 3

In your group, we will call this a "clan council" meeting where you will brainstorm what attributes, duties and responsibilities your clan will provide in building a community.

NINE

CONVERTING DEFEAT INTO STEPPING STONES

Mother Earth

The evening sun cast shadows of color as it began to set in the horizon. Muskwa had just come in from her brisk walk; she loved this time of the year. It was a time she could drink in the varying colors of the landscape with her eyes and take crispness of the air into her lungs. Upon entering her house, she looked at the time and realized her walk had taken longer than she had planned. She had received a dinner invitation from her friend Molay and her family at a restaurant in the city's downtown core. Quickly she darted about to get ready.

Moments later, there stood Molay at the door as beautiful as ever! The two women hugged; her friend always had an inner glow that radiated outwards. Molay's warm and nurturing character drew people to her like a moth to a flame. The two laughed and hugged each other some more. Molay's family had flown in from France a few days earlier and her friend shared how they had never met a Canadian First Nation person, nor were they familiar with the history of Canada's First Nation people. France's information about First Nation people came from a German author Karl May whose writings circulated in the 1800's throughout Europe. In Karl's books he claimed to have had wild adventures on the Great Plains of North America with an Indian blood brother—a fictional Apache warrior named Winnetou. He eventually wrote more than seventy best-selling books that were sought out by avid readers looking to become absorbed in his next adventure. Unfortunately, the writings contained works from Karl's imagination of stereotypical figures of his image of what a "real Indian" looks like, when the writer himself had not met a real First Nation person until he was sixty years old. When Muskwa heard about Karl she felt disappointed, she had spent the majority of her growing up years teaching people around her about the ways of her people because so much of her people's world was misrepresented by disreputable sources. She shrugged the feeling off, as it was time for them to leave. The two women upon their arrival greeted the family, and warm exchanges were made followed by introductions. As the group settled in, each fell into conversations about various things with one another. Minutes moved into the hour, Muskwa watched facial expressions and body movements while members of the group talked to one another. There was a din of quiet to the left of the table that Muskwa had picked up on. She slowly looked in the direction and her eyes fell upon one of the family members who was smiling. The family member's name was Daisy; across from her sat her husband Astra. Immediately she said something to Muskwa in French. Muskwa tapped her friend's arm, and Molay translated the question. The group all fell silent as Molay began to translate the questions and responses between Muskwa, Daisy and Astra. Daisy had wondered what Muskwa's people did in the past to live off the land. With delight, Muskwa shared how her family hunted for moose, deer and goat. With excitement, Astra asked about the landscape, how did they live now? The meat and/or was it plants they ate? If so, what kind? Muskwa had sparked interest in the group and the family listened intently about the use of natural medicines to cure ailments well before the arrival of the Europeans. The group was fascinated, and it sparked more questions. Muskwa paused for a moment, she wanted to make an impact on their learning and to share with them an important stepping stone to healing she had had in her life. Molay would translate Muskwa's story to the group. Muskwa began,

> I twenty-six years old when I was pregnant with my fourth child–my youngest daughter. I remember sitting in the doctor's office, the physician told me I had cervical dysplasia III, a cancer of the cervix. His suggestions were to conduct a cone biopsy of the cervix but it would mean terminating the pregnancy. I was shocked! I did not want to terminate the pregnancy. He warned without the procedure my death would be the direct result of complications. When I left the office I knew one thing for certain, and that was I would find another way. My decision wasn't welcomed by my ex-husband at the time. He wanted what he thought was the best for me, and that was a problem in those days–the doctors knew best! But what if the doctor was wrong? The doctor presented to me alternatives; I could go away get a second opinion OR think about it and come back for a three-month follow-up pap smear to re-examine the cancer cells. I decided I would go to the naturopath's clinic and make an appointment. The following week I entered the naturopath's office and asked Dr. Mountain if he could help. The practitioner was a generous

man; I could see he had passion for helping people. I was twelve weeks pregnant and as he made a list of vitamins I was to take, and gave me a recipe for a douche and instructed me to continue the treatment for three months. I followed Dr. Mountain's advice to the letter. At that time, I also included vitamin therapy. I can't remember if I was scared or not. I can't say that I wasn't because there are fragments of thought that led to the fear of dying that would creep up in my mind. I knew I had to push past it to get well. I returned to the doctor's office for another pap smear when I was twenty-two weeks in pregnancy. Waiting for the results seemed like eternity! Eventually, I got the call and there I was in the doctor's office waiting patiently. As the doctor picked up my chart he read me the results--"negative, no cancer cells." I had never felt more relived in my life! I can remember him saying something like, "There must have been a contamination with the first smear" I knew from that moment in his office there was something to learn about earth's medicine. It had never dawned on me at that my people had been practicing what society called holistic medicine for thousands of years! The experience changed the way I thought about my life! As I walked away from the doctor's office, I went away with not only a relief but a thankfulness I wanted to pay it forward by sharing my story. I had cured my cancer!"

During the translation, Muskwa frequently paused as Molay delivered the story in French. The group sat quietly, some gasped and the rest sat riveted to their seats listening to the story unfold. Astro said, "I don't believe you! I don't believe you cured cancer!" Muskwa looked at him quietly and said, "I did. I not only cured cancer but I saved my life and my daughter's too by making my own decision.

It doesn't matter whether you believe me or not, it happened. She is a woman now, and the experience seems so long ago!" Astro, was one of the younger family members who had learned English in school and could converse with Muskwa easily. He sat for a minutes as Muskwa began talking to another family member about the use of raspberry root, and strawberry leaves. Astro caught Muskwa's attention and said, "I believe you. It's an incredible story; I don't know what to say." Muskwa smiled at Astro and said, "It's ok, I too thought doctors should have all the answers to our ailments. The truth of it is that while they spend thousands of hours studying the anatomy of the body, biology and sciences, they have next to zero for training in natural medicines. In essence, they are trained as health managers and it is up to us to seek out the answers to our health problems. I'm careful here though, as there isn't a replacement for a highly trained practitioner or specialist! Rather, I had become more involved with making my own decisions about my health through the research of alternative healing methods, and combined them with traditional and western medicine.

Astro smiled faintly, and Muskwa could see it in his eyes the overload caused by her story. She had become accustomed to the deer in the headlights look, a look that presented a glazing over of the eyes when news, or information caused an incredulous moment for the listener. It was time for the group to part after their hearty meals. Molay took Muskwa home and as Muskwa entered the doorway of her home, she felt grateful of her health issues of the past. It felt good to share them with others in a positive light.

Chapter Summary

Muskwa's experience that came from her health crisis in her late twenties had opened her up to a whole new journey of exploration with the earth medicines her people used for thousands of years. In this chapter she had shared a personal, and intimate story with visitors from France to help them understand the deeper side of her Native roots and upbringing. Exercise: Read the tables below and choose what interests you, and incorporate them into your life.

Direction	East	South	West	North
Color	Red	Yellow	Blue or Black	White
Aspects of Life	Spiritual	Emotional	Physical	Mental
Elements	Earth	Air	Water	Fire

Four Direction Plants				
Direction	East	South	West	North
Plants	**Tobacco** is used for prayer and offering.	**Sage** for cleansing and purification of negative energy. It is also prepared as a tea to boost the immune system.	**Cedar** is used to purify a person or place. A strong tea concoction poured into a bath relieves rheumatic pain.	**Sweetgrass** is used to promote kindness. A gentle tea concoction is made for the hair
Spiritual	Sweat Lodges, healing & or sharing circles	Meditation designed to promote life forces "prana" into patience, love and generosity.	Subliminal Audio Messages to program your subconscious mind	Mindfulness has its roots in psychology and is to become aware of things in relationship to their value.

Your Turn: Think about four different types of healing modalities you would like to look into. Fill in the chart below. If you need more space, place this diagram into your journal.

Description	East	South	West	North
Example	Drumming or prayer	Attend sharing circle and buy a plant book	Join Tai Chi or Capoeira	Buy an affirmation CD
Your Plan				

TEN

CHANGING BELIEF SYSTEMS

North Direction – Mental

I t was the month of May, early spring had arrived, and at six-thirty in the morning the temperatures had already crawled up to a balmy eighty degrees in Atlanta. Muskwa sat on the patio with her breakfast and coffee with lap top open and perused through her inbox messages. She had arrived in Atlanta the day before to attend a seminar titled, "Experience Your Paradigm Shift." She had heard her guidance mentor on a live conference call with a few hundred people where he talked about his experience being stuck in a belief system. Her mentor's name was Tsi Dene (Rock Man) who described the one belief system that held him in an impover-ished state most of his young adult life. The internal dialogue that he recycled said, "I'm dumb and stupid, I'll never get anywhere without my college education. Oh well, I'll just be a poor janitor all my life." Tsi Dene told the group he realized that thoughts con-trolled behavior and was a form of his own self-sabotaging behavior.

"Guilty people need to be punished and I was doing a good job at that. I realized that if you think you won't increase your income, something else comes along to say something different, and you will surrender to what is familiar to you every time." He said. Muskwa heard him invite everyone to make a leap of faith, and challenge the old patterns of thinking and come to Atlanta! She was a big fence sitter from way back, but with this decision Muskwa decided she was going. She compared a paradigm to Newton's law, "What must go up must come down." In contrast, the law of gravity and motion wasn't so much different than the learning models she had grown up with. Muskwa felt it necessary to look further into some of her patterns of thinking and their origins to free herself from the binding shackles of the victim slavery she had become too familiar with in her life. Muskwa looked at her watch, they would be starting very soon. With the last quick sips of her coffee she straightened her dress as she arose from her seat. Proudly she walked in the direction of the seminar with excitement.

As she entered the doorway, rock n' roll music filled the hall and many of the members were standing by their tables smiling and dancing. Muskwa shook her head in laughter and began to dance to the 60's music. As more songs played, beach balls began to color the atmosphere as they were gently bounced from one table to the other in the air. Muskwa took a few minutes to record the atmosphere with her cell phone to capture the color of the beach balls, people dancing on their chairs, as well as the comradery that created a sense of group connection. The music lowered as her mentor Tsi Dene entered the space to begin with the day's lessons.

As he neared the front of the room, people clapped and he stood quietly for a few minutes. "Welcome, welcome everyone! How many of you have been trained to settle? Too many of us will share our ideas with family or friends, and then accept their reactions as truth.

We make it alright for them to convince us out of our decisions! We then settle!" he said. Muskwa watched Tsi Dene intently, what he said had merit and resonated deeply with her. "We've been programmed to be perfect and to never fail! Nowhere in there did we think about the facts. Fact, there is no such thing as perfect! To who's standards? Who said so? Why do you believe you are worth less? Facts change, and they will only change when we inquire." he continued. "What about smart? If you are the smartest in the group, you need a new group! If we think we're too smart, what we really did was opt out of life's growing and learning. It's a life time endeavor!" he added.

Muskwa sat quietly taking notes, it felt good to hear this man talk. Tsi Dene continued his presentation:

> *"When you were telling friends and family about your dream and they shot it down, how did that make you feel? Quit asking them for permission to live your dream! It's a lie! The early learning model said, 'I'm not smart enough.' Facts change, it was a lie! Your ability to make your own decisions in how you want to make your dream come alive resides within you, not them. Think about the source of your abundance, it doesn't come from you, it comes from God. There is enough for everyone, there is an abundance and if you have been gifted with an idea, celebrate the birth of your idea with the source. Acknowledge the origin of the idea, thank God and ask what will be the first thing you need to do?"*

Tsi Dene's voice travelled through her while she took notes. Muskwa's thoughts recalled her grade five year. The teacher's assignment was for the class to draw a picture of themselves, then color with pencil crayons. While she was drawing, she had noticed how the light had hit her peer's hair and from memory used a yellow colored pencil to highlight the hair in her self-portrait. The teacher marvelled at her drawing, and pointed out how well Muskwa had done. After the teacher left the class, her peers began to bully and made fun of her drawing. "You don't have blonde hair, you don't even know how to draw!" From that time she internalized the embarrassment and anger as, "I can't draw, and I'm not good enough." Later on she hid her drawings, and felt embarrassed when someone discovered them. She realized the hurt became so internalized that her self-worth in the arts had become affected by the belief. It pooled off and affected her self-confidence, and her ability to compete in exhibitions or make any money selling her art work as an adult! While she filled an application to exhibit her work in Times Square, Muskwa recalled her hesitancy. The past inner-voice returned, "What? You think you're good?" She dug for its origin and found it! When she discovered the belief came from her grade five school days, she pushed past it and said, "I am a professional visual artist!"

Muskwa was jarred back to the present when her mentor's voice loudly said, "Don't challenge possibility! Challenge limitations! This is your birth right! Say it aloud, this is my dream!" Tsi Dene waited for the people at each table to stand up and say altogether, "This is my birthright, this is my dream!" Now I want you all to sit and get comfortable. I am going to take you through guided imagery. Some of you might not see things but you may sense the images of your vision, just go with it. Now, I want you to place yourself five years from now. I'm going to ask you a couple of questions, then I will become silent as you draw upon the canvas of your mind, your dream. Imagine a life you'd love to live, what does it look like? Where are you ? Where does it start? See what you are wearing and take in everything around you. What is it that you want, and how did you get it? Feel the successes, touch the rewards and take in all this dream has to offer to you.

Muskwa drifted quietly into outer space, she felt relaxed in her chair. She smiled as Tsi Dene's voice became fainter, and her dream unfolded. At first there was a business woman all dressed in a black dress suit, black heels, with eloquent First Nation beadwork around her neck and in her ears. She saw the woman speaking confidently, freely without difficulties, and as Muskwa ventured closer to her… the woman became her! She felt the warmth of the lights upon her forehead, and a few feet in the subtle darkness she could make out the faces in her audience. There were hundreds of faces, and then a hum as a screen lowered to the back of the stage. Muskwa's microphone was clipped to her shirt, the music began – it was rock n' roll music. She snapped her fingers, danced freely to the screen and in front of it on a small desk a set of brushes and paint. In her vision she saw herself dance painting to the rock music. She painted a giant picture in the dark blues she so loved, of a full moon setting. The audience held portable iPads and half way through the show, they too could digitally add to the painting. No impoverished thoughts existed, images of financial wealth flooded her senses. "It's time to come back," came the voice from Tsi Dene. Muskwa slowly came back to earth and had never felt so self-sustained like this ever! It was truly an empowering exercise. When Muskwa boarded the plane the next day she felt the subtle shift within herself. She felt whole again.

Chapter Summary

In this chapter Muskwa shared her experience in changing her learning model into a positive self-sustaining pattern. A paradigm is a pattern or system of beliefs that come from very early programming we received as children. By five years old, our mental, emotional, and spiritual states have become fully developed. Our learning model creates problems with self-fulfilled prophecy later on in our adult lives.

Examples

Self-Fulfilled Prophecy Statements	Struggles related to	Trigger or Reaction to compensate for struggle
I'm not smart enough	Success	Bragging
I'm not good enough	Love and Acceptance	Lying
I'm a black sheep	Belonging	Abandon people first to prevent abandonment
I'm not as pretty or handsome	Self-Image	Become competitive
I don't fit in	Self-Confidence	Avoidance of people
When people are around me bad things happen	Self-Worth	Avoids intimacy and close relationships
I grew up on the wrong side of the tracks	Financial, Acceptance	Compares self, perfectionism
I don't feel safe going to town	Safety Local	Isolation
I don't feel safe travelling (Fear of the world)	Safety Global	Minimize or Completely avoid travel
I'll never get anything right!	Reality, Reason	Stops trying, accepts
I am crazy!	Self-Worth	Believes he/she is psycho, life on psych drugs etc.
There's something wrong with me!	Self-Worth	Find abusive relationships to support belief
I am a failure	Self-Worth	Blame others for faults

Exercise

What you believe about yourself prevents you from experiencing successes and joy in your life. Practice letting go; the story of letting go is powerful! In society we are not taught how to let go, we are taught how to be go-getters. *"Your dream wants all of you! It's selfish, and it wants you whole."* Paul Martinelli said. Identify one area from the "Example List", or write down one of your own that you want to breathe awareness into. It's time to let go of the woundedness, you no longer have to keep a book of all the bad things that have happened to you. Identify the resentment, its origin and begin to let it go. Facts change, and your dream wants all of you!

ELEVEN

SEVEN SWALLOWS

Morning Star

As the sun began to rise, the darkness of the horizon took on a hazed and greyish color. On the branches of the trees the birds began to awaken, each singing their song as the morning light slowly filtered upon the landscape. Muskwa had arrived during the evening for her fire ceremony held by her teaching grandmother. In the private space given to her, away from everyone else, she spent the night reflecting on her life and sending prayers into the fire. Each time she released hurtful thoughts, or her woundedness she had offered tobacco to the fire in prayer. The morning had been crisp after the night's coolness. She wiggled her toes from underneath the blanket and stretched her arms above her head. As she rose from her seated position on the chair she greeted the rising morning sun. Muskwa gave thanks for Morning Star's lessons of light and guidance. "Such a beautiful orb. A tiny yet reflective planetary radiance to greet the eyes as the color of the morning sky slowly rose," Muskwa thought to herself.

Approaching the fire, she offered the spirit a gift of tobacco. The night felt long but she felt rewarded with personal insights for her journey. As she stood before the waning fire her thoughts drifted back to portions of the night, when she watched the flames dance about in the fire pit. There was an image that emerged within the flames that appeared to be a person kneeling at the bedside of the sick. Muskwa recalled the brilliant ambiance of the flames that turned into a mother's womb where all knowledge began, as a seed.

The image was so real for her, and it stayed with Muskwa. Her heart felt heavy when she thought about her "mother," who had recently gone into the spirit world. She stood quietly by the fire, a tear stung her eyelid. She prayed, *"God, or Creator, I know my mother has gone to a good place. A place alongside my late brother in the heavens with you. I really miss her, I wish I could phone her, and I guess I can. Can you send me a message? A message I would only understand from her to let me know she has made it to heaven? I know I need to strengthen my faith, but at the moment I am grieving and I am struggling because of the anger, hurt and the life I feel she left too soon."*

A few minutes later she raised her head from prayer and looked at the horizon. The ominous threads of light touched the landscape, the colors of the leaves began to emerge as the light filtered through the crevices of the once dark places of the forest tapestry. The silence was broken at her elderly teacher's arrival as she removed the cedar trail in indication of the fire ceremony's end. As Muskwa walked up the pathway she was greeted by other members who had stayed overnight to take in the night's sharing circle. After a good breakfast and some coffee, Muskwa and three others left the house to return to the fire and give thanks. Each walked together side by side to the fire area. The fire keeper was cleaning up around the site when the group arrived.

The four of them laughed and talked quietly around the fire area when Muskwa spotted a small swallow swoop over them, and then it disappeared. The others had continued in conversation unaware of the visit from the winged one. Muskwa watched the sky quietly for the little birds return. The little bird returned with a partner, both danced and flitted about and above the group's head that caught everyone's attention. Gasps of surprise came from the group as they wondered what species of sparrows came to visit. All of a sudden while the group debated on the type of sparrow species, one swooped down from the western part of the sky and almost flew into the fire! Everyone silenced as they began to watch the sky for the next set of antics from their sparrow friends. Muskwa screeched and the heads of the group turned up towards the sky to make out what Muskwa had spotted. A total of four sparrows glided and swooped gently together, then were joined by a fifth. When out of nowhere the sixth and seventh landed on the ground not six feet from the group. The two were feeding on something, in the sunlight a small strip of color on their wing hinted a metallic blue. Muskwa recognized the identity of the bird as a "tree swallow." The visit from the winged ones was short, they left as quickly as they arrived. In curiosity Muskwa approached the place where the birds had been pecking on the ground. The ground was dry, there were no signs of ants or insects which made her ponder further with more questions.

The four continued their discussion, one of the group members said, "It's as if they were bringing a message. We almost lost one birdie as it swooped into the fire! And I've never seen birds come so close to a group of people in my life!" Muskwa smiled and said, "I am trying my best not to read into it in the same way my family would interpret it. See, if an animal or bird does something out of the ordinary or acts strangely, it means bad news is on the horizon. I choose to see this as a normal visit from the winged ones. I had been missing my late mother…" Muskwa paused and looked at her friend White Wolf who was in the group. "You and I have similar losses, you have had a mother who left for the spirit world too. I imagine Creator sent us this message because I had prayed for a message." She said.

White Wolf and the two other women came beside Muskwa and the group hugged one another. They left the fire area to prepare for their journeys home. Muskwa packed her things as the images of the "seven swallows" stayed etched in her mind. She remembered reading an article about the written passages of the Bible, and its alignment with specific numbers. The number seven in genesis 7:2-4; Revelation 1:20 denoted the number seven signified completion or perfection, and was often called "God's number" because He is the only completed one.

For Muskwa, attending Catholic catechism when she was a child taught her how to pray and the value of prayer. Later on in her life as an adult, after visiting various religions and faiths, spirit brought her home to the traditional practices and belief systems of her people in spirituality. In spirit, the recognition of all living things meant to be unconditionally open and receptive, without judgment of all religions upon the earth. To be receptive to the wisdom contained in others, as well as to the writings of the Bible. For Muskwa, in her grief she had lost the connectedness she felt through the messages from the universe.

Muskwa approached her vehicle with her luggage, hand drum, and blankets. She was a different person than the tormented soul she had been prior to the fire ceremony. From her recollection, other members had shared dramatic experiences and profound releases while they were beside the fire. For her, the experience was a subtle shift in her consciousness, so gentle were the changes within her that she would be unaware of them for quite some time. She held onto the feeling of peace that had engulfed her, the presence of love that filled her heart and self-acceptance of her individuality.

Getting into the car she heard the whispers of spirit, "I AM you, I AM SPIRIT." Muskwa marvelled in mankind's ability to pray to God, or Creator or Spirit. She realized all humans struggle, and it is in that struggle that faith can stand up to the storms of life, or weaken from the torrent of life's tests. The experience by the fire and the visits from the tree swallows deepened the roots of her belief system. Her connection to the infinite source, its existence was because of her foundation from a renewed hope and faith in the divine.

Chapter Summary

Muskwa's grief and loss of her mother presented challenges in the belief of heaven. A normal grief pattern for most people. Embodied in pain and sorrow, she opened her channel of reception to spirit through prayer. The arrival of "seven swallows" (tree swallows) had arrived in camp, a message she took as one from her late mother to help comfort her grieving heart. Her late mother's message was, "I have completed my human journey. I am perfect, I AM with the divine, I am love." My dear reader, if you have lost a loved one, no matter what faith you hold, every language includes the word "heaven." Those that have entered the spirit world, some call "angels", are there for us in another form.

Exercise

Create a supportive environment for yourself; either complete this exercise on your own, or invite others to join you. Look at the questions provided for you in the image below. In Muskwa's culture, giving thanks and the release of pain are done in prayers at the fire. Complete this exercise, and within a few days or a week plan to burn this exercise in a camp fire to "let go." As you release it into the fire, send your prayers of gratitude.

Level 5: YOU~ What do you want others to know about you?

Level 4: SMOKE~ As the smoke goes upward to Creator, what will you do to let go?

Level 3: NATURE~ What has helped you on your grief journey?

Level 2: FIRE~ Describe your grief journey.

Level 1: EARTH~What values govern your life?

TWELVE

THUNDERBIRD MEDICINE

West Direction – Physical

It was late June, shortly after the summer solstice. A torrent of rains had covered the borealis forest and the landscape was brighter with newly opened wild flowers. The early morning hue radiated from the tree line a hint it would be another hot day. Muskwa's cousin had phoned her on the weekend to tell her soap berry bushes were laden with berries ripe for the taking, which sent her packing her camp gear. The first few hours in the early morning Muskwa packed, while selecting food for her cooler, collecting harvest buckets, boots, tent, a change of clothing and rain gear. She had become wiser in her older years; a hot day could suddenly turn into brief showers or a heavy downfall of rain.

Once all her camping equipment was prepared, she was driving on the highway searching for the marked turn off. Muskwa spotted the sign on the left where she turned and after a few hours of twisting, winding gravel roads, she saw her dear friends White Wolf, Speaking

Eagle and Dancing Horse waiting on the side of the road in Dancing Horse's red pickup truck. After Muskwa parked her vehicle, the group exchanged warm hugs then proceeded into the bush to scout out the coveted soapberry bushes. For the Tshilqot'in people. soapberry was called Nuw̃ish (no-wish), and a small handful vigorously whipped in a bowl with a bit of sugar made "Indian Ice Cream." Her family knew the healing properties from the plant were used for stomach problems, and berries rendered down the juices created a rich elixir and was a highly sought after trade item by the coastal people. Muskwa remembered her auntie's story about the Carrier Tshilqot'in's trade products on the "Grease Trail" were the bottled elixir or the Oolichan oil. Trading didn't stand still as it crossed over the mountains into Bella Coola where dried salmon also was added to the list. The trade system of her people was more involved and its intricate trade path went all over Canada and into the United States.

The four in the group laughed, visited, and took small breaks during the soapberry harvest. At lunch, the group chose a small clearing to sit and relax as they ate their packed meals. Muskwa loved the time she spent with her friends, it felt good to share past travels and connect with one another through laughter, an essential part of Native life. Her ancestors or eswidan (è-swi-dan) took advantage of the get-togethers and used them as teaching tools. It was a time for the adults to role model leadership to children, tell stories that encompassed protocol, a way to act, proper behavior, acceptable conduct and survival techniques. Women and their little girls went out together to harvest berries, leaves, roots and bark for healing medicines. It was a time when women taught their daughters about the moon cycles commonly referred to as menstrual cycles and/or menopause by the western society. Discussions created support and direction for women's physical changes and training around medicines that would alleviate discomfort to heal the body on all levels.

Thousands of years of knowledge passed down from one generation to the next was almost wiped out by genocide, but now was quietly coming to the surface. The collection of wisdom, nurturing, and teaching, fostered strong foundations for communities in the past and she knew the building blocks for tomorrow were being placed once again by her own active practice to keep the knowledge alive.

Muskwa recalled her mother's story about the boy's training. A boy was a part of the women's harvest until puberty. During the year of a boy's voice change, his mother sent her son out running as the sun rose in the east to jump young saplings. He was to continue running until the sun lit the day, and return to camp. The boy was assigned his own cup, bowl, plate, fork, knife and spoon to clean after every use. He was to prepare his own breakfast, drink room temperature water and resist the temptations to gulp his food. Eating food had to be a ritual, it was believed his hunger would never be satisfied if he wolfed down his food. Running towards the sun every morning meant he would grow as a tireless runner in his adult years. After his year of training, when his vocal chords changed he would have a deeper voice. It was a time for him to join the men's circle to learn how to hunt, track wildlife, and to fish.

The hottest part of the day arrived, sending temperatures in the bush to an all-time high. The wind barely shifted the heat, it wafted upon Muskwa's face, and the insects challenged her ability to continue to pick soap berries. A tiny black fly landed on her shoulder and smarted her with a quick sting as it punctured her skin. "Ouch!" she yelled. The humidity was relentless, she noted the slight shift in the temperature and how the subtle breeze made the poplar leaves flip, so she knew a thunderstorm was brewing.

The group decided to sit underneath a small canopy of pine in the shade located within a small clearing. Once again they laughed about their growing up years, teased one another, and shared memories of travel. Muskwa commented on the humidity and wondered how big the impending thunderstorm would be later on in the day. Her friends looked at her then shrugged their shoulders. Muskwa then shared a story:

"I remember when I was around five years old. My late brother was around three years old, as we were eighteen months apart in age. We had been in the house all day, and my mother had had enough of our fighting and bickering. Outside we were sent. There was an old metal wash tub, and the two of us decided we would turn it upside down onto the ground. We looked around in the yard for sticks, as we were going to copy the Indians by singing like Indians of the past. At the time we did not know that we were Native. We must have seen a Wild West show on our black and white T.V. set and came up with the idea from what we watched. We started to bang on that old wash tub, acting out a make believe song that consisted of a repetitive chorus that sounded like hiya-hiya-hiya-hey – bang, bang, bang on the tub. After a few minutes we were in rhythm, it started to sound good. The memory is so vivid to me because of what happened next! We sounded so good I demanded we sing louder. As I tell you the story, I'm thinking I probably initiated the idea and then like a child, intuitively lined up with the elements. I had seen clouds slowly rolling in, they were dark billowy shapes above us. As we continued to sing, drumming louder I recalled telling my late brother to drum harder! We then heard it. A small rumble, it was thunder! Hit harder I yelled, when all of a sudden a torrent of water fell upon us! The two of us still banging, a roll of thunder and light followed. Then the ambiance was broken when I heard our mother screaming at us. I don't remember being scared of the

thunder until we heard her voice. "You're wet!" she screamed as we came into the porch. Each of us received a slap on wet bottoms, punishment for not coming in sooner. Later on in my travels, I shared this story with an elder from the east. He said, "You sang in the thunderbirds!" followed by his laughter.

Her friends listened quietly, and as the story was digested, there was a moment of silence. Finally, the quiet was broken by Dancing Horse who recalled a time during his growing up years. *"I was ten years old heading home on my bicycle when a thunderstorm occurred. I was cycling as fast as I could! As I rode I could feel the electricity run through the rubber grips on my handle bars!" I made it home safely but the experience sure rattled me!"*

Speaking Eagle chimed in with amazement, "You're lucky to be here!" Then the two talked about the electrical exchanges in atoms, and the distances coming together to create a charge. Muskwa jumped into the conversation excitedly. She said;

"There was one other time I don't know what to truly make of it. But since we're talking about circular electrical charges created in a thunderstorm and its intensity, I can understand how this experience might fit for three kids playing outside just before lightening hits. My late brother and I had gone to visit our friend Ireland who was two houses away from our own. We were outside playing hide-an-go-seek, completely oblivious to the sky getting darker, and it wasn't too long into the game when a gentle trickling of rain started. There was a low rumble above us, when we decided to go inside of our friend's house. We weren't allowed inside our friend's house and looked around for a dry place to continue our visit. The rain became heavier, Twin Eagle and I didn't want to go home. Ireland spotted an

old truck hood propped against a large pine tree not far from the house. The three of us neared it, and quickly decided all three of us could wait out the storm by huddling together under it. We crawled under just as the thunder above us sounded and the earth shook under our feet! We all screamed, and began to talk to one another excitedly! During our discussion all we heard was a loud noise then BOOM! The truck hood got hit by something, the loud reverberation of metal singing…I grabbed my ears OUCH! My brother screamed, and Ireland shot out from underneath the truck hood crying. Twin Eagle and I were right behind, we were very freaked out kids! Ireland was grabbed by his mother at the door, and she slapped him! She told him to go to his room with his lies about being hit by thunder. As the mother yelled at Ireland, I remember holding my ears because they hurt so badly, and all I could hear was a loud buzzing, her voice was hardly audible. As she yelled she pointed to the door. With my late brother Twin Eagle by my side crying and me holding my ears, we hurried back outside. We were terrified; all I could remember was talking soothingly to calm my young brother as we held hands hurrying through the rain towards home. With the rain plummeting down onto us, we arrived home soaking wet, and we each received a spanking for telling a lie about the storm. To this day I'll never forget how bad my ears hurt and the fear around what happened. If the electrical center was under the truck hood, I surmise the outward expansion of it would gradually weaken to zero by the front door of the house. With conduction somewhere outside of the truck hood, I am truly amazed we survived! I can now appreciate the reasons a person shouldn't be out in the open during a thunderstorm! I'm so glad the three of us didn't leave the space when the lightening hit the truck lid!

Come to think of it, the only formal training I received as a child about thunderstorms came from my father who was born and raised in the prairies where electrical storms were nastier than in the borealis of Canada. During a thunderstorm, me being the oldest, was given the honor of covering all the mirrors in the house with a towel or blanket. The explanation? To prevent lightening from seeing its image in the mirror, resulting in a bolt of lightning coming right through the window! We closed all curtains, shut off all the lights and no one could have a bath or be near water till the storm had passed!

While the four sat telling stories, the group noticed a cool breeze and decided it was a perfect time to continue picking some more soap berries. As each of them fanned out, Muskwa found a beautiful bush laden with ripened berries. With a stick she banged lightly, knocking off some of the riper berries. She sat down and started to pick berries off the branches of the plant with her hands. While she was diligently harvesting, she began to think about her friend Ireland. Muskwa recalled his mother had very little patience, and she suspected Ireland's mother was physically abusive to him. She realized her friend Ireland wasn't safe at Serpent Creek Street, and its realization was not uncommon for her as well.

Muskwa reflected back to those early school years, as she was one child who was unable to process information as fast as her peers. In her first grade, she recalled a blurry image of her writing her A, B and C's on a green chalk board in the hallway of her home. Her father was adamant she would learn how to write properly, and he frequented her daily after school assignment. The memory so clear, her father pointed out the letter "A" was upside down. After he erased it angrily, she attempted to rewrite the "A" with her left hand. He slapped her hand, "Use the other hand," he demanded.

In school, she was the tiniest of children. An obedient and quiet child who walked pigeon-toed and became bullied on the school ground. For the first two years of her schooling she had an accent, no doubt her First Nation tonal roots would show up! Instead of "the" she said, "dah". In the early day's teachers loudly used learning problems of children as examples of "what not to do" to the rest of the class. The teacher's projections of her speech inabilities were followed by classmates making fun of her homemade lunches, her newly sewn clothes made by her mother, and the color of her skin or hair.

As she sat amidst the abundance of soap berry bushes deep in memory, she recalled having two Christian friends who also didn't fit into the wider classroom clique because of their religious belief systems. Throughout her school years she tried to fit in, and time and again she was not accepted by the typical "classroom clique." By the time she was fifteen years old she became comfortable with "being different." Her attention was riveted back to picking soap berries. Muskwa looked up at the sky, it had darkened. The cloud shapes and the variety of blue colors found her reminiscing about her eastern Sundance teacher from the "Thunderbird Lodge." His teachings about the "backwards people" had such a big impact to her life and changed her completely. The Ojibway referred to oddball characteristics of a person to that of a teaching trickster, and the Sioux called him or her a "Heyoka." It is said those who didn't fit societal norms, were attracted to the thunder beings of the west, because this was their place in the community. Their abilities resulting from traumatic events in their life such as those of her father's schizophrenia, or her late brother's clumsiness, her late mother's talent in reading minds – all considered strange to most, were welcomed as teachings. Within the traditional communities he or she would be compared to a clown in a positive manner. When the thunder beings come, they arrived in a thunder storm, and each time their wings moved an electrical charge was released. The electricity bolt to crash down upon the ground as a charge swept all negativity away to recharge earth's energy field. For the "heyoka", truth arrived in the representation of one who wears two masks – one for sadness and suffering, the second one for laughter – but both are contained within the same mask. Sometimes they are called the "looking glass people" and their gift is to bring healing to their communities. Muskwa's teacher's wisdom handed down from his grandfathers for thousands of years, created a space for people who did not fit into the label "normal," those who were severely abused, rejected by family or society, or for those who just didn't fit anywhere else.

Muskwa grinned widely, the fear of the dark, walking pigeon toed, tripping over everything, clumsiness, incorrect grammar usage and a host of other imperfections that prevented her from achieving what others called "normal" or being "perfect" were welcomed in the eastern circles as a gift. All her life, her imperfections were unacceptable to main stream society. There was even a ceremony for the medicine that the trickster brought to the communities. A celebration only conducted in a certain place by an adept teacher who was raised and trained in the teachings from the time he or she was a child. It was a time when she recognized the importance of the seven laws, one being humility, "*We are never less than our neighbor or better than him/her either. Everyone has a gift, and it is discovered when the journey is taken.*" The wisdom gave her new meaning: life isn't a competition, we are all equals upon this planet Mother Earth.

Above her the thunder began to rattle. Muskwa quickly picked up her bucket of soap berries and joined her friends as they returned to their vehicles. The group jumped into the red pickup truck, and although squeezed for space, they continued conversations until the rumble of the thunder caught their attention. From the vehicle they watched the thunderbirds (mystical eastern bird) light up the sky, followed by a sonic boom as they imagined the wings contracting, then expanded outwards with a trail of light. The show reminded Muskwa of an old black and white reel-to-reel movie with the flickering of faint light to a bright flash just before the sound of thunder. She gave appreciation to the energy that would ionize positive charges into the atmosphere. There was nothing like the smell from the landscape after a thunderstorm, she thought. Afterwards, she and her friends would find a place to pitch their tent and bed down for the night. Muskwa knew setting up camp after a rain would be a challenge, but she looked forward to the warm glow from the fire, the evening tea with supper, an extended visit with her friends, and an early morning harvest of soap berries before their return to the hustle and bustle of the city.

Exercise

Group – Decide on how many you want in one group. In order for this exercise to work, you will need a minimum of three people. The larger the number of people for this exercise, the more effective the learning will be for everyone. Each group may need to give a bit of distance between themselves and the other group to avoid clashes in noise.

Choose One Person to be a Drill Sergeant

Role is to be shout out directions, speed and accuracy of instructions. Give your group direction, "go right, step ten paces forward, go left and stop." Mix the directions up, interrupt the progress by yelling "that's not right! Do it again!" In the next set of instructions relay them fast, do not hesitate. When the group gets the instructions right, tell them, *"Excellent work everyone but you'll do better next time."*

Group

Instead of wearing your shoes on the right way, wear them on the opposite feet—backwards. Then wait for the drill sergeant to give directions.

Activity

Drill Sergeant – record your observations of the group in your journal. What are the feelings you had and what you would do to in a leadership role to foster change for "drill sergeants?"

Group – record your visual, auditory and participatory observations that resulted from the drill sergeant experience. List the feelings that surfaced and what you would do in changing an environment conducted by a drill sergeant. Are there positive changes you could incorporate? What are they? Briefly describe how this will help the drill sergeant become aware of his or her role, and the changes you would need to make in yourself to become the agent of change.

Nominate one person from each group to share thoughts, and any take away from the activity with everyone in the room.

On a flip chart, write and then underline categories to fill in responses from each group presenter:

East: Spiritual – personal beliefs and or values

South: Emotional – feelings

West: Physical – body

North: Mental – thoughts

Don't forget to include

Solutions or any "aha moments!"

THIRTEEN

WRAPPING THE BUNDLE UP

Moon

Wrapping the Bundle Up represents a summary of each of the chapter's messages for the readers. A "bundle" is a term used by Canadian First Nation to describe a sacred wrapped package consisting of various items such as rocks, crystals, or anything else that possesses spiritual value or of a teaching to the one who owns it. The lessons from women, told by women, and transported down through the generations of grandmothers, seeks to guide women in picking up their bundles. You have worked hard, discovered twelve lessons and grown from your journey while following the chapters in this book. Like the cycles of the full moon, each lesson a hall mark in moving forward from a past paradigm that once held you, to feeling present and looking forward to the future—if just a little bit more than when you started out. Muskwa encourages the men in going back to their circles to heal, and become an altruistic being outside of the patriarchal structure. The analogy of the moon for the thirteenth chapter is about taking stock of the lessons, placing them in your thinking bundle and moving forward on your journey.

Chapter 1 – Full Circle – Respirator & Silver Swans (Mother)

Muskwa relives one of the most tragic days of her lives; the day her mother "Red Tree" passed away from a severe pancreatic infection in a hospital in Kamloops, BC. The author shares her emotions though her character and comes to conclusions that are relevant for anyone who want their lives to have meaning. Muskwa reflects back on some of the key points in her life and acknowledges how they have contributed to her own development into a young elder. She comes to peace with her mother's spirit as she communicates with her, minutes before her passing.

Jorg Schlagheck
Author, visual artist and professional handyman
Contact: Jorgschlagheck@gmail.com
Websites: secreativ.com, jorgschlagheck.com

Chapter 2 – Running Down the Corridor (East Direction – Spiritual)

Reading this chapter on Muskwa's experiences, reminded me of many stories similar to that of what my mom has shared with me, example "The out of body experiences". Which has taught me that there are some happenings which can't be explained through science but rather needs to be felt through spiritual understandings. Understanding that we have a connection to the spiritual world has allowed me to be open minded to different happenings that may confuse those who haven't.

I am fortunate enough to come from a home where we explore our spiritual connection, where the teachings of our past ancestors are recognized and utilized. As a youth care worker, I work with many young individuals that come from homes that have experienced culture loss through assimilation efforts and have never regained that part of their identity. I see the confusion they battle with daily through their delinquent behaviors and actions, having no understanding that part of the pain they carry is inherited from the past, along with feelings of not belonging or positive identity. It took Muskwa decades to understand her own connection to the spiritual, and once she did she was able to turn her "curse" into a "gift", and in turn heal. Now if Muskwa had someone to teach her about her power and her identity as a child, instead of being taken to the Residential school, it may have not taken her so long to find peace. And I think that's something today's youth is lacking, the cultural teachings and understandings from older people to help them resolve conflicts within themselves. The older people could share the bridge of understanding that they are special and powerful in their own rights, and that these powers are gifts and not burdens that need to be suppressed through the use of substances.

Randi Lynn Candline
Education: Aboriginal Mental Health Diploma, Bachelor of Indian Social Work Degree
Employment: Youth Care Worker with Eagles Nest Youth Ranch, Cultural arts and Powwow dance instructor

Chapter 3 – God in Addiction? (Dawn Star)

Muskwa said it herself that "She made a choice to break the cycle". Muskwa shared her story around addiction and how she grew up with it along with her brother, Two Eagles. She shared bits and pieces of his story through his letter and experience in treatment but came to realization they had their own separate stories about growing up in addiction. Either story had a huge impact on Muskwa and Two Eagles. It was the road they chose that separated them but also brought them together.

Ruby Squinas, Roots Practitioner
Kamloops Aboriginal Friendship Society
r_squinas@hotmail.com
250 457 1521

Chapter 4 – Dirty 30's Father (Father)

This chapter provides a delightfully written insight to understanding our past and the effects it can have upon us today. Barbara has shared this so effectively through the story of Muskwa. As a counselor, my goal is often to help people understand the belief systems they have developed over their lifetime and how those beliefs affect their current lives. Without this understanding it is difficult to make positive, lasting changes.

Secondly, Barbara addresses the need for forgiveness. Without forgiveness, we are tied to the past. Often forgiveness comes as we are able to see past our assumptions about another individual's behavior. When we gain an understanding of the "why" it helps us to come to the point of forgiveness. The story provides this through Muskwa's determination to understand her father better. Understanding is the first step to both personal growth and forgiveness.

This chapter is well written and leaves me wanting to know more about Muskwa.

Naomi Deutekom M.Min.
Author of: Humility, Love, and Unity: Reflections on the Book of
Philippians. naomideutekom@gmail.com

Chapter 5 – Witch Doctor (Grandmother Within)

This is a time of healing, a time to journey, a time of learning and acknowledgement. It is also a time of peace within. A time of embracing the beautiful grandmother within, the medicine woman within and of the awareness around the teachings of parents, and those of the grandparents that helped Guide Muskwa's life. Through these lessons, she was guided back to health and healing, and reconnected with Mother Nature. The church and residential schools were a part of a lie and denial of our true strength as a people with Mother Earth. While Muskwa acknowledges the damages caused from the Indian Act and the betrayal from the religious and political structures upon her people, she holds the vision of health and wellness of herself and her family. Through all the hurt and pain of life's journey she is coming home. Home is a peaceful place, with the warm, comforting smells and sounds from childhood spent with her mother and grandparents. She is hearing her Inner Grandmother… Clearly! Thank you, thank you, thank you.

Marilyn Baptiste
Xeni Gwet'in First Nations Government
xenicouncilbaptiste2013.18@gmail.com
Council Member

Chapter 6 – Finding My Circle (PTSD) – (Woman)

This chapter gives an understanding of how our conditioning and circumstances growing up hugely impact how we think and feel and why we act the way we do. Muskwa put herself in a safe environment and began the journey of self-discovery. We don't need to live with lack of self-worth, self-limiting belief and fear. Fear is a belief system that wants you to remain in status quo. But challenging what we believe about ourselves and creating a new level of awareness by developing our mindset will help us towards the life each of us desire and deserve.

Karen Maxwell, Certified Coach/Trainer
Website: www.empowermentmentor.com/karenmaxwell

Chapter 7 – Ordering In (The Child Within)

There's a deep yearning to understand who we are and recognize how we arrived at this point in our lives. In this chapter, we gain a short sense of the life experiences that have lead us to today. The memories of our childhood shape a big part of who we are. Whether positive or challenging, it created the fabric that makes us today. We have a true potential to use all of it to make us stronger and appreciate the opportunities in our life and maximize our happiness. The author brings you through a range of your own emotions as you reminisce on your experiences and recognize how they lead you to where you are today. I enjoyed the opportunity to work through this and look forward to so much more!

Maricela Messner
Speaker, Trainer & Coach
The John Maxwell Team
maricelamessner@me.com
(301) 302-5966

Chapter 8 – Broken Arrow
(South Direction – Emotional)

This was an interesting read. Very different perspective but I enjoyed it and agree addictions if left unaddressed can limit you. It's our responsibility to BOLDLY address them and give them the proper attention when we see anything less. I admired Muskwa's boldness to stand up for her values regardless how hard it was. We should all be as BOLD as her. Otherwise, we're condoning those behaviors and we can never expect change. As a leadership coach and expert, this chapter will encourage your clients to developing a growth mindset.

John Wayne Mullins
Leadership Development Coach and Consultant © 2016
john@johnwaynemullins.com
614-314-1684

Chapter 9 – Converting Defeat into Stepping Stones (Mother Earth)

Seeking life from Mother Earth. Knowing that she will provide and offer the strength to live. The chapter explores and shares how natural medicine strengthened the body, mind and spirit. The teachings exist within us and within Mother Earth. We have the ability to heal our body.

Amber Weasel Head
Visual Artist
Piita-Kihiw Productions
ambercita.wh@gmail.com

Chapter 10 – Changing Belief Systems (North Direction – Mental)

The chapter discusses ways in which old paradigms can affect the way a person views his or her current reality. These old paradigms have the potential to dictate who the person becomes and can influence paths taken in life. For example, as a result of bullying from peers in grade school Muskwa doubted her ability to become an artist. This had a grip on her self-confidence and in participating in exhibitions or furthering her career as an artist. However, Muskwa was able to overcome her challenges once she realized in her adult life the source of her fears. She learned through coaching how to face those fears and discovered the strength to continue her journey. A mentor who had traveled a similar road of limited beliefs helped her to shift her paradigm in order to create a world she deserved.

Bola Disu
Instructional Leader/Staff Developer of Learning Leaders International.
Contact: bodisu33@gmail.com

Chapter 11 – Seven Swallows (Morning Star)

Seven Swallows, the significance of faith in our connection with the Divine. This spoke mightily about the preciousness and power of faith. More precious than gold – Spiritual forces seek to rob us of our faith during times of trial and testing. As gold is refined by fire, so our faith is purified during trials. The seemingly premature loss of a mother is a trial of enormous proportions. But even this trial cannot unseat our faith when we turn to our Creator for help. Our faith pleases Him; it is made perfect in Him.

Thomas Dixon
Certified Coach, Teacher, and Speaker Partner, The John Maxwell Team, Owner,
Greenhorn Advantage
Contact: thomdixon11@gmail.com

Chapter 12 – Thunderbird Medicine
(West Direction – Physical)

A poetic contrast between imperfections as they are viewed in first nations culture versus how they are seen in western society. Through the description of a medicinal berry picking trip the writer describes how getting closer to her native roots "healed" her vision of herself by transforming her from a misfit into a teacher. She describes how the differences she portrayed are viewed as qualities when examined under a different set of rules than that given to us by common western authority figures. She helps us to heal our own self-images, and to see our imperfections in our beings and in our histories, as gifts.

Jessica Byron
Arborist
Sure Wood Tree Care – 289-990-9918

APPENDIX A

The numbers on the shell correspond to each chapter

1. Mother
2. East-Spiritual
3. Dawn Star
4. Father
5. Grandmother Within
6. Woman
7. The Child Within

8. South~ Emotional
9. Earth
10. North~ Mental
11. Morning Star
12. West ~ Physical
13. The Bundle

There are 28 small outer sections to represent the 28 days of the moon.
The 13 larger inner sections represent the 13 moons.

Names of Characters

Big Rock – Father

Red Tree – Mother

Twin Eagle – Brother

Wild Sunflower – Grandmother

Wolf – Great Grandmother

Rainbow Woman – Oldest Daughter

Morning Star – Youngest Daughter

Tsi Dene – (Rock Man) – Teacher

White Wolf – Friend

Speaking Eagle – Friend

Molay – Friend

Ireland – Childhood Friend

Disclaimer

Some names and identifying details have been changed to protect the privacy of individuals.

The information in this book is meant to be a self-help supplement, it is not intended as a substitute for the medical advice of physicians nor replace, proper counseling or medication. The authors and publisher advise readers to take full responsibility for their self-development and know their limits in healing themselves emotionally, mentally, spiritually and physically. Before practicing the skills described in this book, be sure that you have surrounded yourself with support networks like family and friends, and do not take risks beyond your level of comfort.

ABOUT THE AUTHOR

Barbara M Derrick

Arts Leadership Consultant/Coach
Native Studio Art
bderrick@nativestudioart.net

Barbara Derrick who lives in Edmonton, AB Canada is Tshilqot'in from Xeni Gwet'in First Nation Government, located 270 km outside of Williams Lake in traditional territory called Nemiah Valley, B.C. During the writing of her first co-authored book "First Lady Nation: Stories by Aboriginal Women Volume 4; Chapter 3 Muskwa Walks, Barbara's mother passed away. With the thoughts of her mother's trauma from residential schooling and that of the missing and murdered Aboriginal women in Canada it became important for her to lead the way in creation of a new legacy for the women in her family. From the teachings of various grandmothers throughout her life the author has molded and crafted the lessons around her life's experiences through a young elder Muskwa (bear). These lessons will be used as content for the courses she'll develop and for a curriculum she plans to bring to those who are open and receptive to personal growth and development.

Walking in Your Own Power is Barbara's professional working bundle consisting of stories that she has shared with various audiences as a teaching tool to inspire, motivate, and nurture the people around her. She has been known to empower those she loves to not only dream it, but become it. With ten years of Social Work background, and another fifteen years of instructing in the Native traditional arts she has followed a calling to open her own art studio business so that she can continue expanding her passion in the arts, share her leadership training, and help make a difference in other's lives.

In her knowledge bundle, Barbara holds two years of university, and four separate certificates in: Native Social Development Worker Program, John Maxwell Coach, Speaker & Trainer, Native Arts & Culture Instructor, and in Teaching Adult Learners. Notably the last two certificates she graduated with distinction, the highest marks in her class.

Barbara Derrick is available for workshops, retreats and speaking engagements based upon her book *"Walking in Your Own Power."* Want to get to know Barbara better go her website at: *http://www. nativestudioart.net.* You can contact her with any questions at *bderrick@nativestudioart.net.*

Works Cited

Frank, L. R. (2005, June 26). *Electroshock: A Chronology of Psychiatric Abuse*. Retrieved from End of Shock: http://endofshock.com/history.htm

Maxwell, J. (2016). *John Maxwell on Creating a Legacy*. Retrieved from Preaching Today: http://www.preachingtoday.com/illustrations/2005/september/16127.html